ANTHONY LOWELL
TUCKER STIPE

HOW TO TRADE

Earn 5.7% per month, trading only 10 minutes per night, using Hedge Fund manager secrets that they don't want you to know.

Dedicated to my beautiful wife Mary.

As I lost money learning how to trade the wrong ways you stuck by my side. As I made money trading the right way you stuck by my side.

Are you serious about controlling your financial future and living the life of your dreams, now and in retirement?

Then this book's for you.

Want to be wealthy?

Start by thinking and acting like you are and doing what the wealthy do. The wealthy take risks, but very calculated low risks. Join the prosperous minority who make sound moneymaking decisions every day while trend trading the financial markets.

Let me explain how you can take minimal risk, spend only a few minutes a day and still bank more profits than most professional stock brokers (and certainly more than when you let someone else manage your account).

Hello; my name is Anthony Lowell and I'm a full time trader. I've learned a lot in my many years in the markets and want to give you some of that knowledge.

As you will see from reading this book and from viewing your free video course at *www.howtotradebonus.com* that not only am I a full time professional trader, but that I can help you become one also.

I've written this book to introduce more people to the idea that they can take control of their own financial future. You will notice I pull no punches. Some say I am blunt, but the truth is just call it the way I see it so I can sleep at night.

I don't like financial advisors who charge you 1-2% management fees while losing your money.

I don't like the hype "trading gurus" that run infomercials and spam your email box. If anyone could make 50% per month like they claim they would be running the largest Hedge Fund on the planet and making billions in performance fees, not teaching.

Our low risk 10 minute per night system usually makes a few percent per month (unless you learn our option strategies which increase your potential exponentially) which can equal over 5-6% per month with compounding. As you will learn, the keyword is low risk. **Having a low risk system is the ONLY WAY to have long term compounding work for you.**

I want to show you that no matter what the over-all economy is doing, you can enjoy more freedom now and retire securely when you choose, not when the government tells you you're entitled to and then only at poverty level *social security* check.

If you're the kind of person who enjoys the freedom that comes from taking responsibility for his own finances, or even if you'd like to, but aren't sure that you're capable, please join me as I explain what's involved, who the players are and how you can seize the wheel and guide your own economic ship safely and confidently. I know, once you've read this book, you'll be ready to set sail on one of the most exciting and lucrative adventures you've ever dreamed of.

Helping You Retire On Time,

Anthony Lowell

P.S – My motivation in writing this book was not about being a "published author" or "trading guru." At my age I have nothing to prove, nor an ego to feed. Life and trading has been good to me. My hope is to be able to give back a little to others my years of experience. So, if you are expecting a polished book you will be disappointed. I am a professional trader, not a writer. If this bothers you and you feel more comfortable learning unproven fake strategies from an infomercial "trading guru" then go ahead and put this book down now. But, if you would rather learn from a real trader, who won't hype you up, or a fancy marketing company or professional author then read on.

Also you won't see a lot of charts in the book because I've placed most of them in the bonus website.

I would suggest before you get sidetracked go register for our free training videos and advanced money management software at www.howtotradebonus.com

CONTENTS

CHAPTER 1

Why You Must Take Control of Your Investment Portfolio NOW.

If early retirement is important to you learning to trend trade stocks and ETFs is the perfect low risk opportunity for you to do so. Real quick, put down this book before you get sidetracked go register for our free training videos and advanced money management software at *www.howtotradebonus.com*.

Nobody really cares

It's a bit of a cliché but it's true: NO ONE cares more about your economic security than you do. OK, maybe your spouse cares as much as you do, but certainly no professional financial advisor or money manager does. There are plenty of good, ethical advisors who will do the best they can, within the system they work under, to guard your funds and get you market average returns. But when they go home at night they're not spending any time thinking of ways to improve your retirement or how to get your kids' college tuition banked before they finish high school.

The head of the company you work for doesn't care. He's busy taking all he can out of the company now, including an increase in his pension annuity, while eliminating your pension. The Employee Benefit Research Institute's 2010 Retirement Confidence Survey reports that over 50 percent of workers say they're counting pension benefits among their retirement funding sources, though only 21 percent of current workers in the private sector have traditional pensions, and many of those are underfunded and could be wiped out with a bankruptcy. Government workers are much more likely to have a defined benefit pensions, but state and local governments (who can't print their own money like the feds) are warning that those are also severely underfunded and may start cutting benefits.

Who's the sucker?

The industry referred to as "Wall Street" certainly doesn't have your best interests at heart. For most of us, the game's been rigged so we have to play at their table and they get to deal every hand, and you know what they say: If you can't spot the sucker at the poker table, it's you. If you're a business owner, you can set the rules for your own deferred compensation plan (you have to abide by the IRS rules the Wall Street guys helped the government set up). Still, you get all the market risk and precious little of the reward for saving in your 401k/457/403b and/or IRA.

How about the government – surely they're interested in protecting honest taxpayers from financial destruction, after all, we pay their salaries, right? Well, unless you've been out of touch over the last 10 or 12 years, you've seen how the government protects the average investor.

Enron was the darling of Wall Street during the 1990s; it was named by Fortune Magazine "America's Most Innovative Company" six years running. They seemed to create new markets and money out of thin air. It began to look more like hot air in 2001 when the whole house-of-cards came tumbling down leaving stockholders, bond holders and employees holding worthless shares in a giant fraudulent company. Investors were fed false information while insiders sold their shares, passing the losses on to the public and the employees who held the stock in their pension plans.

But the Securities and Exchange Commission has the power to make brokers and money managers act in their client's best interest right? Well, just who they consider it their job to protect is a question we should all be asking after seeing the extent of the Ponzi scheme Bernie Madoff, a former chairman of the NASDAQ stock exchange, ran for twenty years.

During that time he contributed at least a quarter million dollars to political campaigns and curried favor through the trade group, Securities Industry and Financial Markets Association, where he and his brother Peter served on the Board of Directors. A former assistant director at the SEC is now married to Madoff's niece, and Madoff has called SEC Chairman Mary Schapiro a dear friend.

If the stock market crash of 2007 and 2008 had not caused an unusually high amount of redemption requests, would we have ever found out about the giant fraud before Bernie Madoff died? Probably not! But since the government runs an even bigger Ponzi scheme, called Social Security, it's unlikely we can expect any help from the regulators.

It started as a good idea – let's force workers to save some money and require their employers to put in some too. Then, when they reach the last few years of their life and are unable to work, they won't be reduced to poverty. But, as Thomas Sowell, a noted economics teacher and writer explains,

> "***Social Security has been a pyramid scheme from the beginning.*** *Those who paid in first received money from those who paid in second — and so on, generation after generation. This was great so long as the small generation when Social Security began was being supported by larger generations resulting from the baby boom. But, like all pyramid schemes, the whole thing is in big trouble once the pyramid stops growing. When the baby boomers retire, that will be the moment of truth — or of more artful lies. Just like Enron."*

In 2011, the Social Security system will pay out more than it receives from non-governmental income sources. **This will be the third time the system has gone broke.** The first two times, in 1977 and 1983, the tax rates were increased and benefit age was increased. This time, the government is funding it with interest money it creates from the treasury. As long as the Chinese continue to buy our government bonds, we can continue the charade, but as soon as our bonds are unwanted, the whole system will be bankrupt. If you've been counting Social Security income as part of your retirement plan, stop now because the money won't be there.

Amateurs can't compete

But you're not trained in finance and money management you say? Exactly; and, because you don't have a professional system, you've probably bought into the BHP strategy (buy, hold & pray the money's there when you need it). With no risk management strategy and no way to make money in bear markets (averaging down is a fools strategy), many individuals ride the rollercoaster that is the financial markets and cash out when they can't stomach anymore losses.

Investor psychology follows a fairly predictable pattern as shown in this graph.

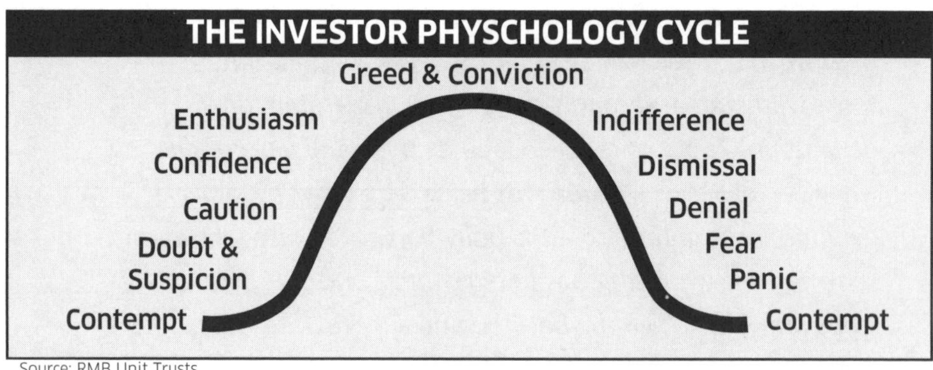

Source: RMB Unit Trusts

At the bottom of a Bear market, we feel contempt. As it begins to abate, we look on the markets with doubt and suspicion, followed by cautious optimism, enthusiasm (buy, buy) and peaking with both greed and the conviction that we are invincible (where most people buy more). As the Bull market crests and begins correcting, at first the investor is indifferent, dismisses and denies the losses before fear and panic set in (where most people sell) and returns to feelings of contempt – we've been fooled again!

Instead of thinking you'll outsmart your human emotions, face the reality and make a plan to mitigate the damage. Instead of following those emotions, follow a systematic, mathematical plan with pre-set buy and sell prices. You'll still feel the emotions, but you won't base your trading decisions on them. Plus the longer you trade a mechanical, rule based system the less emotional you will be in your trading.

In case you don't know almost all online trading brokers now offer free demo accounts (paper money accounts), so you can practice as long as you want without risking a dime.

For a list of our favorite brokers register for our free bonuses at *www.howtotradebonus.com*

CHAPTER 2

Yes! I'm Talking To You: Saver, Investor, Trader

Before we go any further, let's define some terms. In today's financial system, the individual can be a saver, an investor, or an active trader.

The Saver:

Who transfers a portion of each paycheck into an account that pays a small amount of interest and, at an FDIC bank, the principle is guaranteed. No US investor has lost any principle (up to the insured amount) at any US bank since the depression of the 1930s (before the FDIC was established). **However, with inflation averaging over 12 percent per year over the last 50 years (639.55 percent for 01/1960 – 01/2010 according to the calculator at inflationdata.com)**, your principle is being eroded if you're getting the average savings return over the same 50 year period. Here's a chart of savings returns from 1987 through 2005: Is your return any better?

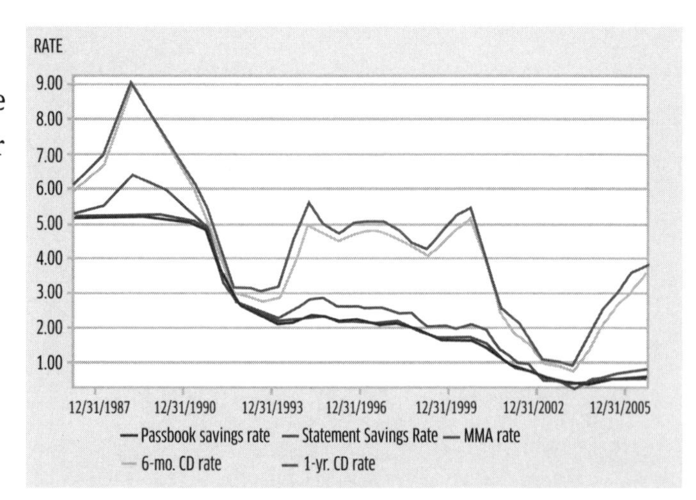

The US government has basically declared war on savers. It needs to stimulate the economy, boost business activity, and lower unemployment and by saving money, you don't directly support this agenda. Instead you earn interest by allowing the bank to use your money. To persuade you not to save, the Federal Reserve has set interest rates at zero percent (at the time of this writing) because the bank can borrow from the federal reserve at less than zero (when inflation is factored in) so they don't need to pay you any interest.

You get essentially no reward (except safety of principle) for saving money. Since the Fed is inflating the money supply asset prices continue to rise and your savings future purchasing power declines.

The Investor:

The Investor takes some of the money he's saved (or received via gift or inheritance) and seeks to increase it by participating as an equity partner or bond (debt) holder in publicly, or sometimes privately, held businesses. Time horizons vary, but a minimum of three to five years is often suggested. This is the arena where most of us were taught to use the BHP (buy, hold and pray) method. Investors usually enter a position without a stop-loss, often pay large management fees and hold portfolios that are so diversified they will never "beat" the over-all market.

Because most people do not have any training in choosing companies or even industries to invest in, the Mutual Fund industry has grown up to service the investors. We'll explore the pros and cons of Mutual Fund investing shortly but for now, let's define a trader.

The Active Trader:

The Active Trader uses the financial markets to capture gains for their own portfolios by harnessing the inherent volatility of the financial markets. Instead of buying an equity and holding it for years, sometimes decades, hoping the market price rises (and possibly collecting dividends), the trader buys or sells anticipating a short term price change. A trader has clearly defined parameters and adheres to a plan that incorporates the potential movements the market can make during his time horizon. He sets stop losses and exits or shorts losing markets. He can make money whether the general market is moving up or down.

There are many types of trading; scalping, day trading, swing trading, position trading and many more. I day traded 10-12 hours per day for almost 10 years and now prefer to have a life. That is why I trade the daily charts which only requires about 10 minutes per night.

CHAPTER 3

Why ETFs instead of Mutual Funds?

Whether you're an investor or a trader (or a little of both), I encourage you to switch from using Mutual Funds and individual stocks to Exchange Traded Funds (ETFs) for your financial market transactions. Much of this book is about ETFs, but since our system works on anything that produces a chart (stocks, forex, options, futures, commodities, etc.) Therefore, I decided to simply name this book, "How To Trade."

An ETF is made up of a basket of stocks that trades on an exchange in much the same way a stock share trades. They combine the simplicity and liquidity of an individual stock and the diversification of a mutual fund. So an ETF trader can access the potentially high returns of individual stock trading with the benefits of diversification and sector selection that a mutual fund provides.

You know exactly what you're getting.

Mutual Funds are only required to reveal their holdings quarterly. Just prior to the end of the quarter, many fund managers participate in a game called window dressing where they sell their losers or equities that do not match the fund's stated objective, and buy the winners or correct equities for the particular fund. As a shareholder, you may never know exactly what's in your Mutual Fund at any given time.

ETFs holdings are established at inception and rarely change. You always know exactly what equities, in what amounts, comprise an EFT.

But, with Mutual Funds you get:

At the top of the list are high fees and a lack of liquidity. Even if you choose a no-load fund, the managers have to be paid. There are a variety of fees that are deducted before the Mutual Fund's returns are calculated even if you pay no loads or even transaction costs.

By definition, Mutual Funds' buy and sell orders are fulfilled only once a day. At the end of each trading day, the closing prices of the fund's holdings are tallied up and divided by the number of shares outstanding, to calculate the fund's NAV or net asset value. Then the orders that came in during the day are processed using the NAV.

In theory, all buyers and sellers receive the same price, but some funds have been exposed for allowing large institutions to front-run their common owners and make trading gains at their expense.

Many funds limit an individual owner's transactions in a direct effort to discourage trading. Mutual Funds, whether run legitimately or not, do not allow the individual investor to participate in the market gains available to traders. With Mutual Funds you will never realize he full profit potential of trading the markets.

If you'd like to know about the history and problems with the Mutual Fund industry, download our free article called Death of Mutual Funds in your bonus section: *www.howtotradebonus.com*

You will find to be an eye opening article that you won't be able to put down.

ETFs allow the individual to trade like an institution.

You buy sectors instead of individual companies so you participate in market moves without subjecting your portfolio to the day-to-day gyrations of any one company. You suffer almost no individual company risk because the EFT's basket of stocks is less volatile and the price changes are more predictable.

Because ETFs trade all during the market day (and some after hours), the ETF trader can chose exactly when to enter and exit a trade. Since **there's always a trend** to trade in some part of the market, the ETF trader can be consistently adding to his assets.

In the ETF market, we can short the market or particular sectors, **even within an IRA or 401k** (by using inverse ETFs) allowing us the potential to make money no matter what the overall market's direction.

Since an ETF is a group of equities, the price gaps between order and execution are minimized and the manipulations (like institutions and Hedge Funds who hunt trading stop-loss orders) are greatly reduced when compared with trading individual stocks.

The ETF trader is in control

ETFs allow you to control when you take capital gains/losses and you always know what those amounts will be. You, the trader, choose when to trade your ETF and know immediately what the tax implications are so you may offset a gain or make other corrections.

Mutual Funds capital gains/losses are calculated based on all the shares that were traded during the period. Your fund will send you a 1099-DIV after informing you of the amount near the end of the calendar year. You may be forced to report gains, and pay taxes on them, even if you did not realize any personally. The sad thing is that many of you reading this already know this because it happened to you!

Five reasons you're NOT a good candidate for ETF investing:

1. You have only $50 a month to get started.

   Without at least a moderate starting stake, the transaction costs for buying very small quantities of an ETF will consume your gains and even eat into your principle.

   There are Mutual Funds that allow you to open an account with $100 and put as little as $50 a month into them or just open a savings account at your local bank. Come back to ETFs when you have a minimum of $5,000, to make the trades worthwhile. On a side note, yes you can use our system to trade e-mini's or forex and open an account with only $500, but once you get up to $5,000 I recommend switching to trade ETFs as they are lower risk.

2. You want to invest in individual, mid to small cap, international companies.

   While there are many non-US options for ETF investors, the equities they hold in foreign companies tend to be large-cap. It's unlikely you'll be able to bet-the-farm on a small, up-and-comer using an ETF.

3. You want to invest in the broad market with no regard for sectors or segments.

   While you can buy broad market ETFs, the real power is in the ease of crafting a strategy that changes as the economic climate changes. If you don't want to be even remotely involved in the management of your money, you don't need to bother learning about ETFs. Just let a professional manage your holdings. Of course if you lost 30-50% in the 2008 crash I'm sure you will think twice about this. I believe by the end of this book and our bonus video course you will never be a buy, hold and pray investor again.

4. You want to set it and forget it – your horizon is infinite and you don't want to make any adjustments once you invest.

   Same comment as #3. The real power for individual investors in using ETFs is the ability to respond to changing economic and political trends. But if you are really set on this course of action at least download our FREE report on ETF sector rotation that **only takes two minutes per month that has tripled the returns of the S&P. Once again it can be found at: *www.howtotradebonus.com***

5. You may need the money you place in a thinly traded sector or regional ETF to cover an emergency or other expenses.

   Some ETFs trade continuously and some are rather thinly traded. No one (that I know of) recommends you put short-term money you may need to cover emergency expenses, or planned expenses occurring within the next 6 months, in any kind of equity investment. The possibility that you'll have to sell at an inopportune time, combined with the transaction costs, make the safety of a Money Market or savings account the appropriate vehicle for your cash cushion.

CHAPTER 4

ETF Basics: The Who, What, Where, When and How of ETFs

Who Created and Sells ETFs

The first fund called an ETF was traded on the Canadian exchanges in 1990. In 1993, the first US exchange traded ETF was the SPDR that replicated the Standard and Poor's 500. Asian markets followed in 1999 and the European in 2001. In 2008 the industry changed when the US Securities and Exchange Commission begin allowing actively managed ETFs along with the more common index fund.

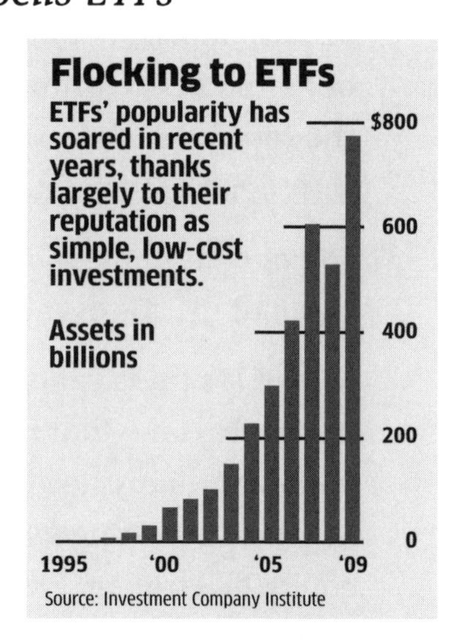

The industry is dominated by Barclays Global Investors (the originator of SPDR), SSgA, The Vanguard Group, iShares and now Mutual Fund giant Fidelity.

Since ETFs were born in the information age, they're able to take advantage of technological advances and financial market innovations and are shaped into any form the markets desire. And yet they're very stable with the original SPY still the most widely held and traded fund. **As of 2011 over 1 Trillion dollars is now in ETFs.**

What exactly is an ETF

An Exchange Traded Fund is an open-ended fund that holds publicly traded shares of equity, debt or other financial assets. The fund trades separately from its underlying assets, but the spread between the market value of the fund's assets and the fund's price is usually quite small. Unlike Mutual Funds, another class of open-ended fund, shares of an ETF trade on the markets.

EFTs are registered with the Securities and Exchange Commission (SEC) with the institutional creator buying and placing the underlying assets in the fund and then selling shares of the newly created fund. The owners of the ETF shares are free to trade their holding during regular market hours (or by any other legal means), but they cannot require the institutional sponsor to liquidate the underlying assets and redeem their shares (as, technically, Mutual Fund share owners can).

ETFs are often described as a hybrid of Mutual Funds, individual equities or debt instruments, and Closed-End Funds. The ETF trader gets the diversification and security of a Mutual Fund and the freedom to buy or sell (including sell-short) like the owner of an individual share of a stock or closed-end fund.

Traditionally, ETFs have very low expense ratios because once the fund is created there is very little management required and most adjustments are made by computerized systems. Since the fund only trades when there is a material change to its underlying assets (for example, a company in the fund is merged or sold or goes out of business), it generally has no capital gains or losses to report. The changes in the value of the underlying assets are reflected in the ETFs market price and the individual shareholder decides if or when to realize gains and losses by buying or selling.

Where are ETFs Bought and Sold?

Authorized Participants, mostly large institutional investors, are the only entities actually authorized to buy or sell shares of an ETF directly with the fund manager. They must buy or sell in what's called creation units which are blocks of shares typically in the tens of thousands, and it's usually an in-kind exchange for baskets of the fund's underlying securities.

The Authorized Participants may be acquiring the ETF shares for their own portfolio, but usually they are acting as market makers, providing liquidity and helping to keep the market price close to the net asset value of the ETF's underlying assets.

The secondary market is where you as an individual will buy and sell ETF shares from the Authorized Participant using a retail broker. It's really not necessary to understand why this convoluted system was developed, you only need to know how it functions and how you can use it to trade the trends and increase your portfolio.

When are ETFs the Right Tool?

We can think of ETFs, especially the narrowly focused specialized funds we use to trade sectors or trends, as power tools. In the hands of a skilled craftsman they help to produce beautiful useful projects that enhance a home. An amateur using the same tools can cut off a finger or ruin his home.

Luckily, almost anyone who's interested can learn to use ETFs safely to produce powerful returns for their portfolio. But chose your instructor carefully; chose one who has successfully and consistently risked his own money and earned real-world rewards, not one who just knows the theory.

ETFs vs. Mutual Funds

Let's compare the features and benefits of using ETFs and Mutual Funds for your trading and investing.

	Exchange Traded Fund (ETF)	Mutual Fund
Buying and selling shares	Through a brokerage account.	Through a mutual fund account or through a brokerage account.
Share pricing	Market price fluctuates throughout the trading day.	Priced once a day after financial markets close.
Transaction costs	Brokerage commissions and a bid-ask spread that's built into the market price.	Brokerage commissions (may be waived).
Trading flexibility	Trades processed any time during the trading day. Limit and stop-loss orders may be placed.	Transactions processed at the next closing NAV (net asset value of fund's holdings)

**All investments are subject to risk.*

While you may have purchased Mutual Fund shares through a broker in the past, you were actually purchasing a share from the fund company. When you purchase an ETF share, you're buying on the secondary market from another share holder. Mutual Funds must allow share owners to cash out (unless their charter specifies otherwise).

CHAPTER 5

Your Investment and Trading Alternatives

I want to be sure we understand the differences and similarities between the most common classes of equity and asset classes we can use for trading and investing. Below is a comparison of three of the most widely available vehicles: Exchange Traded Funds, Mutual Funds, and Stocks.

Attribute	ETF	Index Mutual Fund	Individual Stock
Diversification	Yes	Yes	No
Traded throughout the day	Yes	No	Yes
Can be bought on margin	Yes	No	Yes
Can be sold short	Yes	No	Yes
Tracks an index or sector	Yes	Yes	No
Tax efficient as turnover is low	Yes	Possibly	No
Low Expense Ratio	Yes	Sometimes	Not a factor
Trade at any brokerage firm	Yes	No	Yes

EFTs are the hybrid option. They trade like stock shares while providing the diversification of mutual funds. Their performance closely (but not exactly) tracks the investment returns of the stock, bond or commodity that make up the fund.

ETF vs. Individual Company Stock

Owning an ETF is more like owning a basket of stocks than a single stock. Yes, if you're in a very narrow sector fund most of the stocks in the ETF are going to follow the same trend. But your ETF is much less volatile than any one stock. For example: if you own an ETF that holds pharmaceuticals and one company reports bad news from a drug trial, that stock may drop significantly but another stock in your ETF may go up if they have a competing drug in their pipeline.

So it's easy to diversify some of the risk away without diversifying so much of the potential rewards out of your portfolio.

Buying and selling ETFs is very similar to buying stocks. They trade during the day with sellers offering at a price (ask) and buyers placing orders (bid) at market or a limit price. The transaction costs are nearly identical to stocks with a brokerage fee for each transaction. However, because the ETF's value is a combination of its components, the spread between the ask and the bid prices tends to be smaller than for single stocks.

ETFs, like stocks, can be bought on margin to increase your leverage and they can be sold short. You also incur brokerage fees with each trade, just like a stock transaction. However, some of the big Mutual Fund companies who have started ETFs are waiving fees, so your transaction costs may be lower than with stocks.

Because ETFs are the 21st century's first big financial product hit, you'll find your options expanding almost daily.

ETF vs. Mutual Funds

You probably already have an idea of my opinion of the big Mutual Fund companies but let me explain why I dislike them for wealth building and preservation.

Actually, they do an excellent job of building wealth, for their creators. Fund managers are some of the best paid Wall Street players and, because they generate huge amounts of brokerage fees, they enjoy perks in addition to their salaries and bonuses.

The origins of the Mutual Fund are noble – create a vehicle that allows the average investor to enjoy the diversification of a large portfolio while maintaining liquidity and to spread the fees over a larger volume thus decreasing the individual's costs.

***Returns are not guaranteed*

Some investors believe that because they employ professional managers Mutual Funds are almost guaranteed to increase in value. But, unlike fixed-income products like bonds and treasury bills, a Mutual Fund that holds stocks will fluctuate with those stocks and experience losses as well as gains from the buying and selling that the manager does. Just because the fund employs a professional manager does not mean you can skip the research and risk analysis, just like any other financial transaction.

There's also some confusion about the safety of the fund and the guarantee (or lack thereof) by a government agency. If a fund is dissolved, the investors will only receive the value of the liquidated assets, in proportion to their share of the fund. Since the fund's assets could theoretically become worthless, all your money is at risk. This premise is especially confusing when dealing with Money Market Mutual Funds that attempt to maintain a consistent share value. Do not confuse a money market mutual fund with a money market deposit account at an FDIC insured bank.

Mutual Funds are not FDIC guaranteed. From the FDIC.gov site:

"Securities you own, including mutual funds, that are held for your account by a broker, or a bank's brokerage subsidiary are not insured against loss in value. The value of your investments

can go up or down depending on the demand for them in the market. The Securities Investors Protection Corporation (SIPC), a non-government entity, replaces missing stocks and other securities in customer accounts held by its members up to $500,000, including up to $100,000 in cash, if a member brokerage or bank brokerage subsidiary fails."

And let's talk about diversification.

First off, an ETF offers diversification since it is comprised of a basket of securities, so you do not sacrifice the risk reduction. In addition, since your ETF holdings are always known, unlike a mutual fund who only reports holdings quarterly, you can avoid over-diversification or the risk that your fund manager is piling into today's popular stocks even if they're outside the fund's stated style.

You've heard them – all the experts (valid or not) expounding on the need for diversity. And, like the debacle of the Enron 401k plan showed us, you can never count on any one company, no matter how well you think you know the business, to secure your financial future. But, you can also spread yourself too thin by diversifying away any chance of achieving a meaningful return. If for every winner you have an offsetting loser, at the end of the day you're behind since trading isn't a zero-sum game.

So what exactly do we mean when we talk about diversification? Conventionally, it refers to the correlation between your holdings. By diversifying you are willing to reduce your potential gains to also reduce your losses and lower the volatility of your overall portfolio. This is often achieved by spreading holdings between sectors, consumer vs. industrial, and regions, domestic vs. foreign, that usually move in different economic cycles.

But remember, that **no matter how diversified your portfolio**

is, your market risk can never be eliminated. As the international markets become more open and available and economies become more co-dependent, finding sectors and regions that move up when others are moving down is becoming more challenging. You can still reduce risk associated with individual holdings (called unsystematic risk), but there are inherent market risks (systematic risk) that affect nearly every equity and debt instrument, and no amount of diversification can prevent it.

We have to ask if we even want to diversify away our unsystematic risks. **Risk is measured by volatility.** The more your portfolio moves within a timeframe, the riskier it's considered. Using the statistical concept of standard deviation, optimal diversification seems to occur with 20 stocks in a portfolio.

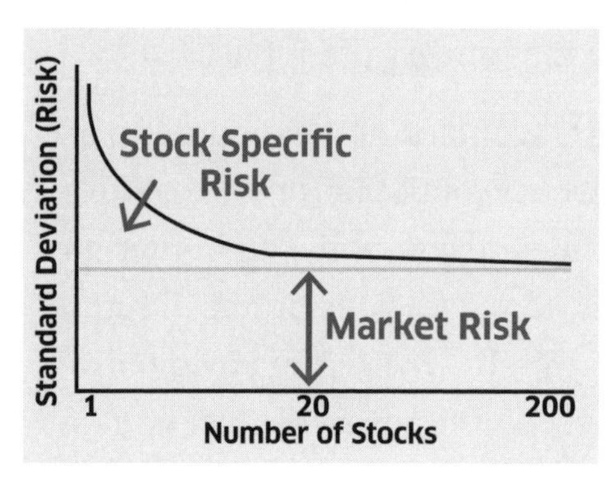

The classic, "Modern Portfolio Theory and Investment Analysis" (love the catchy title) by Elton and Gruber, defines the risk for a portfolio with one holding at 49.2 percent and a fully diversified portfolio (of 1,000 holdings) with 19.2 percent, the market risk we cannot diversify away.

The 20 stocks portfolio has a 20 percent risk achieving 97 percent of the risk reduction while saving transaction and bookkeeping costs.

Many investors have the misguided view that risk is proportionately reduced with each addition to a portfolio, but risk reduction is not a linear function. There is strong evidence that you can only reduce your risk to a certain point beyond which there is no further benefit from diversification.

Simply having 20 different stocks does not get you diversification. The stocks must be uncorrelated so they move in different directions during the different economic and market cycles. Additionally, your portfolio and net worth are diversified by holding assets in different classes. This is why your trading portfolio is a relatively small portion of your net worth, the old "don't put all your eggs in one basket" rule.

For this reason we often use a broad market index ETF to achieve optimal diversification with minimal transaction costs. So, some diversification helps reduce risk, but too much diversification will rob you of returns. The main ways we (traders) reduce risk is by only risking 1-2% per trade, not over trading, not always being in the market, and trading the downtrend when the market crashes.

Using ETFs, you decide how much of your account to hold in cash. A mutual fund must maintain a level of liquidity to handle withdrawals and so they often keep substantial cash in the portfolio. Especially in times like this when cash is paying almost no interest, just being able to use your entire portfolio for income production can boost your returns.

The whole idea behind mutual funds is to employ professional management, but as a fund owner you will have to pay both the shareholder fees and the operating fees. The fund managers get paid regardless of the fund's performance, **in fact when returns are low or negative the fees go up as a percentage of your account.** This further reduces your returns now and in the future since your account balance is reduced. If you were getting exceptional returns in exchange for the fees you could argue for them, but the vast majority of mutual funds underperform the general market and most managers who can generate higher returns have left the mutual funds to run hedge funds.

Mutual funds are only required to keep 80 percent of their holdings in the assets their name and prospectus identify. The fund manager can invest the remaining 20 percent in anything he chooses and even the 80 percent is open to interpretation. A "growth fund" may place your money in any type of equity the fund manager wants to bet on.

This makes evaluating and comparing mutual funds difficult. The basic comparisons of past changes in the fund's net asset value are just that – past performance.

It is important that you understand the problems of the Mutual Fund Industry as an investment vehicle. You can download our free article called Death of Mutual Funds in your bonus section: *www.howtotradebonus.com*

Additional benefits of using ETFs include:

You can trade any time during the market's operating hours and process your order through any brokerage service you chose. If you're using stop and limit orders, you're much likelier to get your orders executed as you planned. You can also use a margin account to buy ETFs, allowing you to take advantage of new opportunities and leveraging your account for even greater returns if you know how to properly manage the margin. ETFs can be sold short which allows you to profit in markets that are trending up and down. Selling short is no more than borrowing a security, taking an order to sell it at a certain price, and then buying one to return to the lender when, hopefully, the price the on the open market is lower than what you sold it for.

If you are new to trading and you are not clear as how to use stop and limit orders or how to sell short, go register for our Free training videos at *www.howtotradebonus.com*.

One of many training videos you will find is "How to use Buy Stop, Sell Stop, Sell Limit and Buy Limit orders."

Side note, I'm a patriot and love my country and need to get this off my chest. Selling the market is not un-patriotic. America was built on capitalism and the markets are a great example of pure capitalism. So buying or selling the market is participating in what made America strong. Also if you are squeamish about others losing money in the market, don't trade, because the winners (us) are only created because losers exit. **Wining traders don't create the losing traders, but the losing traders do create the winning traders.** So never feel bad when you pay the price to learn to trade and go on to make millions.

Using ETFs, we can track almost any index, sector, region or country. This allows us to participate in many different markets where non-correlated trends are playing out, and means there's always a trend we can use to make money. Up markets, down markets, booms, busts, using ETFs and trend treading means we can take advantage of all the opportunities the modern financial markets have to offer us.

We also keep more of our profits with ETFs. Because we're in control of which holdings we buy and sell and when, we can tailor or transactions and accounts to minimize personal tax liabilities and maximize returns by reducing taxes and transaction costs.

CHAPTER 6

Top Mistakes ...

ETF Traders Make

ETFs are a great way for smaller investors to trade hard-to-access market niches or the performance of an index without having to handpick stocks. But there are good strategies for using ETFs and some bad ones. Here are a few of the things you shouldn't do:

... Chasing returns

When tempted to trade based on a tip, media coverage or past performance, examine the technicals and look to see if it is a system trade or not. Also consider whether this particular fund fits into your trading plan – what's been great for your next door neighbor may not be for you.

In my experience most that chase hot tips or stock with media coverage lose over time.

... Trading too much

Yes, I'm an advocate of actively managing your ETF portfolio and setting reasonable stop losses, but it's important to know the impact of too-frequent buying and selling. Doing it as often as you'd buy and sell stocks may result in increased transaction costs and tax issues – short-term capital gains are often higher than taxes on long-term capital gains, so be aware of the bottom line.

... Becoming attached to an asset class

Know when the trend is over. Instead of wasting your time in a fund that's played out and hoping that it will come back, move on to other opportunities. By not doing so, you could be missing out on the chance to be in on a potential long-term uptrend.

... Making assumptions about funds

Investors shouldn't assume from an ETF's name that that's what it holds or assume that just because a fund has the word "global" in the name, it doesn't have a heavy weighting in the United States. For example, the SPDR FTSE/Macquarie Global Infrastructure 100 (GLL) has a 39 percent weighting in the United States. That's not saying it's good or bad, but is that the exposure you want?

... Not starting with a plan

You need a plan before you trade, before your emotions can get in the way and trump logic. Our trading system plan uses a mechanical system with exact entry points, stops and exit targets. Additionally, we set all our trades while the markets are closed, further avoiding emotional decisions.

Stock Traders Make

Lots of the same mistakes ETF traders make. Anyone who's going to trade the markets has got to find and follow a system or plan. A few of us are gifted with the ability to understand the markets and play them profitably, but most of us need a guide. This leads us to another problem many people run into when learning how to trade:

... Following an unproven plan or mentor

Many successful traders make enough money in the markets so

they have no need to sell their programs. They're afraid that if they reveal their strategies they'll stop working (a common problem called slippage). But classically, a trader is a lone-wolf type who doesn't know how to teach someone else to use his system. He stereo typically prefers to sit behind his monitor all day watching the market action and researching potential trades. Traders typically spend every waking hour trading or thinking about trading and have few extra-curricular activities that don't feed into their trading obsession.

How do I know? Because I used to live that lifestyle. Lucky for me, I've been able to learn how to teach our systems, plus I created one that allows me to make plenty of money without constantly watching the markets.

Consequently, the people who sell trading systems typically aren't the trader who developed and tested the system. If a trader wants to sell or teach his system he'll find someone who knows how to market it and sell them the rights to the system. Often he's willing to do that because the market conditions have changed and the system no longer produces the returns he's looking for. Active traders who coach real live students are rare. I don't have time (or the desire) to be traveling around pitching the system in hotel meeting rooms and I don't hire telemarketers to pose as trading coaches. All our coaches are full time traders.

Some of us do enjoy the thrill of teaching others how the system works, and developing a training system is a great way to document your system and fill in any holes you find as you do so. One of my greatest joys is hearing a student say they fired their financial advisor or quit their job.

All traders, regardless of whether they trade options, stocks, ETFs or futures, struggle with two more issues:

... Failing to master the ego

I'm not going to go all crazy on you here but I've known many a trader, professional and students, who let a little success go to their head and ultimately ruin a promising trading career. Once you let go of your ego, it will clear the way for continued education. Refusing to acknowledge mistakes or accept any help or assistance will only hamper you in the long run and prevent you from growing as a trader.

Just being aware of this pitfall is 90 percent of the battle. Having good colleagues who will call you on it is the other 10 percent. By joining a team of traders you can avoid the ego driven blunders and mature into a successful trader. I've been nicknamed "the tough, but loving parent" on my coaching webinars because I will call out and hammer students who break the trading rules by taking profits early, moving stops, risking too much, etc. Would you rather hear what you want to hear or what you need to hear?

You do not have to go it alone. My true success and wealth as a trader and educator didn't come until I humbled myself to the experienced wisdom of a mentor. He not only taught me new things, but corrected those things I thought I knew.

... Talking to the wrong people

Amateurs tend to shout their trades from the rooftops, which can cause them to hold onto a losing position and ultimately lead to a bruised ego once they're forced to acknowledge that a trade didn't work. Experienced traders know how damaging a lack of confidence can ultimately be, so many don't risk talking about their trading to people who don't understand the system.

This doesn't mean you shouldn't discuss anything with others or isolate yourself as a trader. The people around you can be a wealth of information when it comes to strategies, ideas and learning experiences. On the other hand, take what you hear from people with a grain of salt and do your own due diligence before you take a position. Don't always believe what you hear from others, and do what's right for you based on your proven system.

Speaking of proven system, that is why we have two full time programmers on our staff. **I like to run and show students the statistical back test so they can have full confidence in the system before risking a dime.** If a "guru" can't show you statistics don't believe a word they say. If it is a mechanical system (like mine) it can be programmed and back tested with Trade Station or other software.

In addition, it's important not to let your emotions (or those of the media and the general public) to drive your trades. By settling on a strategy that works for you and sticking to it, you can ultimately position yourself for success.

Every successful consistent Trader has developed the mental resolve not to be emotionally moved by the opinions of the media or of others. For you to master the psychology of trading I have included one of our many training videos, "Trading Psychology Tips" in your bonus section: *www.howtotradebonus.com*

Long-term investors make

Our current century hasn't started off so well for investors of all types, and you and millions of others are being forced to rethink their investment strategies just to survive. The markets certainly saw their fair share of volatility before now, but this is different. Times have changed; the old way is on the way out.

... Now is the time to take charge of your money

For most of our lives, the vast majority of us (boomers in the USA) have been fortunate to have many opportunities to improve our personal economic situations. Our homes appreciated in value, our college educations afforded us a steady job in growing knowledge based industries and a continual rises in the value of US companies stocks have all been seen as our birthright, almost taken for granted.

For much of modern investing history, you and countless other investors have heard that buy-and-hold was the way to go. Experts have assured us that, no matter what happens in the markets, they always trend up over time. If you could just hang on and ride it out, you would be duly rewarded with a handsome retirement fund. But the things investors were once able to bank on are gone. **Buying and holding stocks can no longer be counted upon as a sure way to financial security.**

Many of us became aware of the opportunities in the equity markets when discount brokers lowered the barrier to entry and our pension funds became 401ks and IRAs. Until 1975 brokerage fees were regulated the transaction fees added 50 to 75 cents to the price of each share (which usually had to be purchased in blocks of 100) on both ends of a trade. But, Charles Schwab discounted those fees after the 1975 deregulation to $15 per transaction and now it's possible to trade for $7 or $8 each way, and to buy or sell odd lots of as few or as many shares as suits your needs.

... Believing buy and hold (plus praying) still works

If set-it-and-forget-it ever really was an option (maybe for the Robber Baron's trust fund babies), you have no reason to cling to this illusion. First off, no matter what 5 to 10 year period during our lifetime you back test, you're going to find that the market went up and went down. Since stock market participation became more widespread in the last quarter of the 20th century, we've seen a boom-and-bust cycle in most every decade.

If you invested in the S&P 500 in 1997 and held onto it through all the ups and downs until early 2009, you would actually be about where you started (if you had the stomach not to sell during the crashes). This equates to 12 years of holding with only dividends to offset the losses and, you're 12 years closer to retirement.

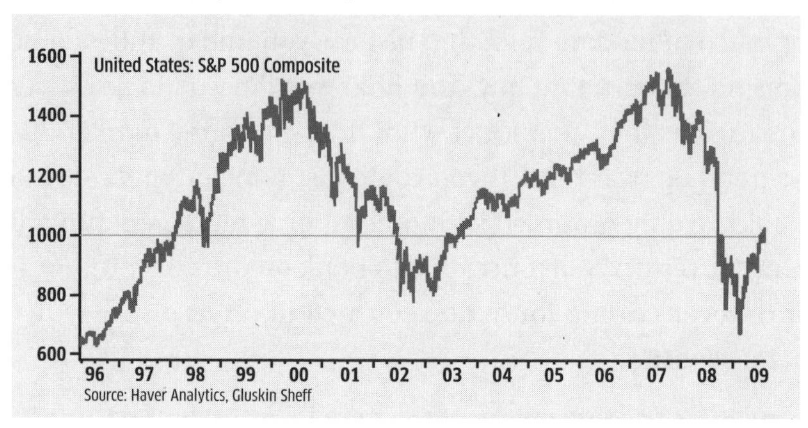

Now is the time to take a more active role in your portfolio by following the trends and using a simple strategy that can help protect you on the downside while having you in the markets for potential long-term up-trends.

What can you gain from all this? You will have peace of mind. You will know how to manage your emotions. You will know that you can make money in any kind of market, and avoid those bubbles, booms and busts that have plagued so many other investors.

... Confusing the marketing gurus who sell advice with mentoring

Since most of us didn't learn investing and trading at home, and even fewer of us were taught the basics of money management in school, once we decide to take control of our financial future we start looking around for guidance. But, because there's a lot of money to be made in the business of investing and money management, it gets confusing real fast.

It's unlikely this book is your introduction to the business of trading and investing. Maybe you have received those letters in the mail touting a penny-stock or a monthly stock tips newsletter. Maybe you've read the stories of modern day legends like Warren Buffet and George Soros (an excellent idea, by the way). But, until you expand your awareness, even get burned a couple times, it may be difficult for you to sort the truth about trading and investing from the hyped-up claims of the investment guru marketers. If you have never traded you are in the right place. I will never hype you up. You will have losing trades. You will be tempted to break the system trading rules. You will have drawdowns, but if you stick to our low risk robust system you can have exceptional gains for decades.

By joining our team of traders you can mature into a successful trader. Yes, I will lovingly hammer you along the way when your ego decides to deviate from the rules of our proven low risk system. I want you to understand how important it is to be part of a real trading community that **supports one another**. To understand not only the content of the support but the motive behind the support you will receive go to *www.howtotradebonus.com*.

Savers make

Does the plan to deny yourself many creature comforts for 50 some working years while saving large percentages of your earnings to live off of during your old age work? It can. But those who are willing and able to ignore the consumerist society and focus on the distant future from a young age are rare.

It's getting harder to compound your way to wealth when the banks are paying you less than half a percent interest on your savings.

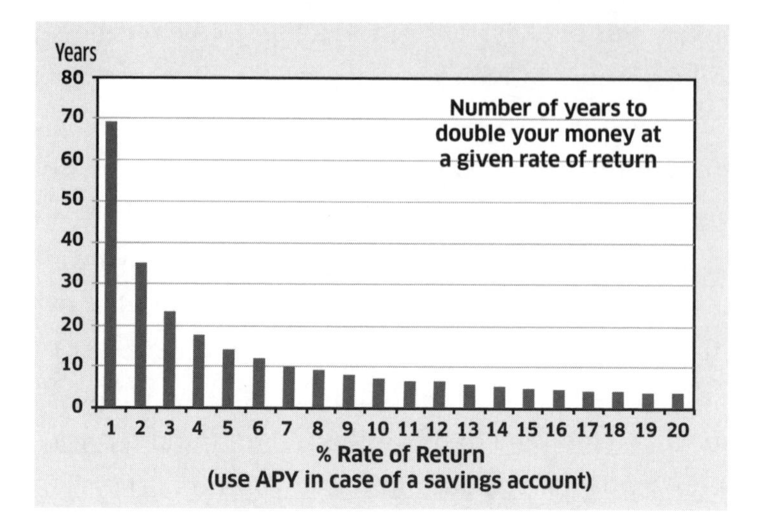

Let's do the math. Take your entire Grandparent's birthday gift money from birth to age 15 and put that $1,000 in the bank. Then, beginning at age 15 you save an average of $500 a month for the next 50 years with a monthly compounded interest rate of ½ a percent. At age 65 you'll have $342,176.21. If you withdraw only the interest in year 51, you'll have $1,714.81 to live off of for the year. (I hope you have another source of income.)

Say you get 2 percent – above the current rates but closer to the average for the last half century. You'll end up with $ 518,380.04 and $10,463.17 or a little more than six times more, but still nowhere near enough to even buy your basic food supplies in 50 years!

You'd need to get that monthly savings amount up to $5,000 to get $104,138.28 to cover living expenses in the year 2060.

CHAPTER 7

Some Truths About Trading the Financial Markets

In order to be a successful trader, you must understand the realities of the markets. You must learn how the professionals make money and what is possible. Most new traders lose a substantial portion of their capital and then quit trading without ever having known what profitable trading is all about.

For many years college professors have argued that the markets are both random and highly efficient. If this were true, it would be impossible to gain an edge on other investors by having superior knowledge or a superior approach.

Professional traders, who make their living trading rather than studying the markets, dismiss these ivory tower theories. For example, George Soros has made billions of dollars from trading and many call him the greatest trader of all time, says:

> *"The [random walk] theory is manifestly false—I have disproved it by consistently outperforming the averages over a period of twelve years. Institutions may be well advised to invest in index funds rather than making specific investment decisions, but the reason is to be found in their substandard performance, not in the impossibility of outperforming the averages."*

Mathematicians have conclusively shown the financial markets to be non-linear, dynamic systems and use chaos theory for analyzing these systems. They can produce random-looking results that are not truly random and chaos research proves that the markets are not efficient, and they are not predictable.

Most beginning traders assume that the way to make money is to learn how to predict where market prices are going next. As chaos theory suggests, the truth is that the markets are not knowable except in the most general way.

In his book, Methods of a Wall Street Master, trader Vic Sperandeo (Trader Vic) warns:

> *"Many people make the mistake of thinking that market behavior is truly predictable. Nonsense. Trading in the markets is an odds game, and the object is always to keep the odds in your favor."*

Successful trading does not require you to effectively predict the future. Good trading involves following trends in a time frame where you can be profitable. **The trend and proper money management is your edge.** If you follow trends with proper risk management methods and good market selection, you will make money in the long run. Good market selection refers to trading in good trending markets generally rather than looking for a particular situation likely to result in an immediate trend.

To learn more about our Low Risk Trend Trading system go register for our free training videos and advanced money management software at *www.howtotradebonus.com*.

There are three related hurdles for traders. The first is finding a trading method that actually has a statistical edge. Second is following it with consistency. Third is consistently following the method long enough for the edge to manifest itself on the bottom line.

This statistical edge is what separates speculating from gambling.

In fact, effective trading is actually like the gambling casino rather than the gambler. Professional commodity trader Peter Brandt explains it this way: "A successful commodity trading program must be based on the simple premise that no one really knows what the markets are going to do. We can guess, but we don't know. The best a commodity trader can hope for is an approach which provides a slight edge. Like a gambling casino, the trader must earn his profits by exploiting that edge over an extended series of trades. But on any given trade, like an individual casino bet, the edge is pretty meaningless."

Unprofitable and frustrated traders want to believe there is an order to the markets. They think prices move in systematic ways that are highly disguised. They hope they can somehow acquire the secret to the price system that will give them an advantage. They think successful trading will result from highly effective methods of predicting future price direction. These deluded souls have been falling for crackpot methods and systems since the markets started trading.

Author Jake Bernstein describes how these desperate traders are victimized:

> *"Futures trading is ultimately very simple. Any attempt to make trading complex is a smokescreen. Yet for self-serving reasons an army of greed-motivated promoters try to make things complicated. Too many market professionals consider it their mission in life to obfuscate. Why? Because in so doing they give the appearance that their efforts are scholarly and important. They create a need for more information, and then they fill it!"*

Books on how to trade are famous for showing a few well-chosen examples where a described prediction method worked. They never show what would have happened if you had applied the method faithfully for many years in numerous markets. Those who have tested these methods have found that in the long run almost all of them don't work. Be wary of any trading method unless you see a detailed demonstration showing that it has worked for at least five to ten years in a variety of different markets using exactly the same rules.

For the person who wants to trade rationally and prudently, they must ignore the promises of those promoting prediction mechanisms and concentrate on finding and implementing a proven, integrated methodology that follows market trends.

CHAPTER 8

5 Ways To Fail as a Trader

It's routinely estimated that at least 90 percent of all new traders lose money. The other 10 percent manage to either break even or turn a profit – and a select few do it consistently.

So what do the 90 percent do that the 10 percent don't do?

First, They Lack a Methodology

I learned early on to be a consistent successful trader you must have a clear mental and concise method of approaching the markets. Guessing or going by gut instinct lands you in the 90 percent losers' bracket over the long run. Without a trading methodology you don't have a way to identify a buy or sell signal and you can't consistently and correctly identify the trends.

How to overcome this fatal flaw? Get a trading journal and define, in writing, what your analytical tools are and how to use them. It doesn't necessarily matter what (proven) system you follow but what does matter is that you know what constitutes a buy signal, a sell signal, where your stops are placed and how you'll exiting a position. Boil it down, keep it simple. If you can't write it on the back of a business card, it's probably too complicated.

Next, They Lack Discipline

When you have clearly outlined and identified your trading methodology, then you must have the discipline to follow your system. If the way you view a price chart or evaluate a potential trade setup is different each time, then you have either not identified your methodology or you lack the discipline to follow it. **The formula for success is to consistently apply a proven methodology.** So the best advice for overcoming a lack of discipline is to define the trading methodology that suits you and follow it faithfully.

Third, They Have Unrealistic Expectations

Yes, it is possible to experience above-average returns trading your own account. However, it's difficult to do it without taking on above-average risk. So what is a realistic return to shoot for in your first year as a trader a gain of 50 percent, 100, and 200 percent? A realistic goal, initially, could be to not lose your capital, to break even. If you manage that, then try to beat the broad market index and then learn to be profitable over the long term.

Be aware that all traders experience losses but that with proper money management you can be a winner overall. These goals may not be flashy but they are realistic, and if you can learn to live with them – and achieve them – you will be a successful trader.

Fourth, They Lack Patience

Any one market may trend only 20 percent of the time, the other 80 percent you must wait for a trend to develop. In any given market and time frame, there may be only two or three really good trading opportunities. Because trading is inherently exciting (anything involving money is usually exciting), it's easy to feel like you're missing the party if you don't trade a lot. So, unsuccessful traders start taking trade setups of lesser and lesser quality and begin to over-trade.

With trend trading you don't have to beat yourself up over missed opportunities because there will be another one tomorrow, next week and next month.

And Finally, They Lack a System for Money Management

This topic deserves more than just a few paragraphs, because money management encompasses risk/reward analysis, probability of success and failure, our protective stops, and position sizing.

The professional traders tend to limit their risk on any given position to between one and three percent of their trading account. If you apply this rule to every $5,000 in your trading account, you can risk only $50-$150 on any given trade. Many traders begin to trade without sufficient capital in their trading account for the markets they choose to trade.

To overcome this problem, you must be willing to abide by the maxim "**aim small, miss small**". If you have a small trading account, then trade small. On your way to becoming a consistently successful trader, you must realize that one major key is longevity. I call this "Staying in the Game". If your risk on any given position is relatively small, then you can survive the drawdowns. If you risk 25 percent of your account on each trade, four consecutive losers puts you out altogether.

Trading successfully is not easy; it's hard work and requires you to develop parts of yourself you may have avoided until now. And if anyone leads you to believe otherwise, run the other way, and fast. But this hard work can be rewarding with not only an increasing net worth but also the sense of satisfaction and freedom you'll feel when taking responsibility of your financial future.

If you redeem the free coupon on the back cover of this book you will receive our free money management and position sizing calculator.

CHAPTER 9

How To Be a Successful Trader

First, understand that there are no free lunches; you get what you pay for.

Second, realize that all traders must pass through the enlightenment barrier before they can win big, and it all starts with superior investor education.

Three traits (all of which can be learned and developed) that are common among successful traders are:

- Confidence,
- Consistency
- Discipline

Almost every successful trader whose results have been documented uses a mechanical trading system. A good system automates the process and makes decisions for the trader to execute. When traders are disciplined to follow the system, they enjoy consistent returns and overcome the fear and greed that would cloud their human emotional judgments if they lack a system they trust.

Confidence in a system allows the trader to overcome fear when losing because he knows the system will be successful in the long-term. The trader avoids emotional mistakes and enjoys the ultimate rewards of a successful system. So what you want is to know how to find and develop confidence in a trading system.

A good system that's followed only sporadically will not be able to produce outstanding results. Building wealth requires that the investor consistently add to his net worth. I'm not saying vacations aren't allowed, but you must be dedicated to implementing your system on a long term, consistent basis to realize all the profits possible.

One of the unique features of our system is that after you have set it up, have confidence in it, and have implemented it on a consistent long term basis, you will be able to make quick after-market decisions and set your trades **in only 10 minutes a night**.

Discipline for traders follows confidence in their system. When the system gives you a signal it is important that you harness your emotions and follow the signal.

In addition, I see several psychological hazards new traders (and some veterans) encounter. First, be wary of who you take advice from and whose opinion of you has value. Friends, family, brokers, even other traders are A) probably not successful traders who understand what you're doing, and B) have their own agendas, fears and phobias.

Next, they either place blind faith in a system without testing it or they're so skeptical of a system they won't test it. Computers and the easy access to historical data allow us to back test and try out a system without investing much money; take advantage of your opportunities.

I really can't overestimate the psychological difficulty of becoming a successful trader. In his book *The Elements of Successful Trading*, Robert Rotella says:

> *"Trading is one of the most stressful endeavors imaginable. Taking losses day after day with a strategy that, just a short while ago was working well, can be a terrible experience. Trading performance can be consistently volatile with good and bad times highly magnified. The market can batter your psyche and gnaw at your soul. These bad experiences will never end as*

long as you trade. The more successful you are as a trader, the more money you will lose."

You must keep your trading in correct perspective and as part of a balanced life. It is an emotionally intensive activity whether you are doing well or going in the tank, and it's easy to let the emotions of the moment lead you into strategic and tactical blunders.

Psychology is a huge part of trading so let's cover some more hazards in the next chapter.

CHAPTER 10

Emotional Pitfalls Can Sabotage Your Trading

A mastery of trading psychology is the difference between the trading pros and amateurs.

To become a conscious and successful trader, you'll combine education, experience and psychological conditioning. It will take time, disciple and the right experiences to see the results you desire in your trading account.

Take a look at this example of self talk when traders experience a loss.

> Trader 1 says, *"Wow, I lost $500. Guess I should have gotten out earlier."*
>
> Trader 2 says, *"Hummm, I did everything according to the plan, followed my system's signals and got stopped out. That's just the way it goes some days; next."*
>
> Trader 1 reacts with a reinforcing negative statement: *"I lost $500."* This demonstrates that the trader hasn't done an analysis of what happened, and he blames himself and reinforces that it is his personal failure, making it emotional by quantifying the loss.

This kind of thinking tells the subconscious, which stores everything, that you lost money and adds an emotional component to the loss. It also causes the subconscious to build an association between a trading loss and emotional distress. Then it files that away and waits for similar reinforcements. Trader 1 didn't learn anything that might help him make better trades, but his subconscious learned that trading is painful.

Trader 2 chose to see the trade in a different way. To him, the loss was just a low but predictable probability occurrence, not a personal failure. It was accepted, with no hint of emotion; it's just part of trading that any system, no matter how positive overall, has a certain percentage of losing trades. His subconscious was told, *"Everything is normal, there's nothing to fear."*

You start by telling your subconscious what you consciously want it to believe as a part of the discipline of following a trading system. It doesn't really matter too much what system you choose, the power and profit is in a disciplined application of proven trading behaviors over a reasonable time. You accomplish this by segregating your trading account from those you use to run your daily life, practicing via simulated trading environment (what we used to call paper-trading), and by interacting with more experienced traders who can help you through the rough patches.

If you believe that trading and the lotto have anything in common, you're unlikely to ever be a successful trader. Most people buy lottery tickets hoping to win a big jackpot, not five or ten dollars, because it's easy to pass up a small profit in hopes of scoring a larger one. The problem is, hitting the jackpot is extremely rare. Traders who win small but consistently don't let profits slip away and tend to come out ahead at the end of the game.

The big "F"

Most of us have a big hurdle to get over since we were raised in a system that graded our efforts and equated failure with worthlessness. Nothing could be further from the truth; in fact, **humans seem to**

learn faster from failure than success. But looking for someone or something to blame for failure won't serve you in trading. Understand that many "successful" (profitable) traders fail more often than they succeed trade-for-trade. It's important to look at trades that do not work according to plan and determine what, if anything, we want to do differently next time, but blaming yourself or someone else will put the brakes on your trading career.

If you persist with an inability to admit and learn from failures, your trading career will be short. No one likes being wrong and for **traders the cost for having to be right is money**. What's interesting is that many folks would rather lose money than admit failure, but being wrong, and taking a small loss, is much less expensive than holding on to a losing position because you feel that the market is going to come back in your favor and prove you right.

Then we've got the fear of missing the party which may be responsible for more losing trades than any other. It causes overtrading and also causes traders to jump the gun and start a trade before the trend is confirmed. If a trade is worth taking, waiting for prices to confirm your analysis will not affect your profit that much and will save you from losing. It's better to be willing to miss an opportunity than to suffer a loss because there will always be another trend to trade.

And there's also the Systems Junkie. Many traders, especially new traders, believe that they can make millions if they just find the right system. Skipping from system to system will guarantee failure because you never allow yourself the time and experience to consistent confidence in it. This also harks back to the inability to admit failure and take a loss, because no system has 100 percent winners.

That's not to say you shouldn't be reading and learning new methods for trading. Successful traders are always watching, adapting and testing new ways to identify and execute profitable trades.

Don't start trading if you don't have the financial and temperamental resources to make it a long-term commitment. You cannot adjust based on short-term performance. A great system frequently has extended periods of losses, and even a broken clock is right twice a day. Don't jump in based on a short string of winning test trades, and don't dismiss a system with a string of losses. It really takes years to properly evaluate a trading system.

If you begin to allow your winners to inflate your ego, when the string of losses comes (as it surely will), you will be devastated and most likely give up rather than suffer through the drought. Consequently, don't allow yourself to increase risk when the system is returning a string of winners, because when the losses come you can easily be wiped out. The best time to increase your trading is actually after some drawdowns but risk management is so critical to trading success that it has its own chapter. To obtain our free money management software go register at www.howtotradebonus.com.

In this chapter it is important for you to be aware of the psychological traps all traders either fall into or avoid.

Speaking of drawdowns, be prepared to feel a little depressed when yours occur, even though I'm doing my best to prepare you for a string of money losing trades. Trading has a lot in common with golf, including the ups and downs and the ego attachment to the outcome instead of the process. You'll have to experience the highs and lows for yourself, but being aware they're coming and what your response should be will help you exert more control. Those who master their own mental game go on to master the markets (and the golf courses).

Managing Emotions

Well, by now you should understand resistance and support, started following your trading system and have learned how to use your trading platform. You may have already made some trades. Some may be winners and others may be losers. At some point in your trading career you will have a hot streak and have ten straight winners. You may also have a losing streak of ten straight losers. Do you know what we call this? **TRADING**

The key to being a successful trader is managing your emotions when this happens and managing your emotions on all trades. Let's talk about that now. Everyone has emotions. When you lose a loved one or close friend you go through an emotional process. We are all human and that is a very natural human thing. Everyone reacts differently. Trading is no different. There will be times when it is emotional. In trading most times emotions are generated by fear.

You will hear people tell you to manage your emotions. I have even used the phrase with our members. I think that is wrong. My point is you can't just shut down your emotions. What you really need to do is manage how you react to your emotions. Let's talk about some ways and tools to help you manage the way that you react to your emotions.

One way is to master a trading system like the ETF Trend Trading system. Mastering it is just part of the process. You also need the discipline to follow the system. If you are using the ETF Trend Trading system you already know that we eliminate the emotions. We do this by deciding on trades and setting up our trades after regular market hours. Setting up trades when price is not moving helps you take emotions out of your decision process. We also know our maximum loss before we setup the trade and set a stop loss at that price. We do this by using our "Risk Per Share" formula in conjunction with knowing the maximum account percentage we are willing to potentially lose on each trade. Once again, we know what our maximum potential loss is before even entering the trade. This way if you get stopped out there are no surprises when it happens. Yes, there could be times where there is a gap overnight and you end up losing a little more than you thought. There will also be times when gaps happen in your favor. The main thing is you are out of the trade based on your original plan.

Most traders that do not use or follow a system stay in losing trades too long and get out of winners too soon. They also move stops and targets discretionarily, instead of following their system. You are not any smarter after you are in the trade. If anything you are dumber, because now fear is a part of your decision process. There is only one reason this happens. You have let your emotions start managing the trade instead of knowing how to react to the emotions and keeping your emotions out of the trade. As I mentioned earlier, everyone handles their emotions differently. Learn what works best for you. Maybe it is a breathing exercise or listening to music. Whatever it is that you use it to get back into the comfort zone use as soon as possible. Once you are there, now you can react without fear and emotions.

Another way to minimize emotions in trading is to trade financial instruments that match your trading personality. If you are more comfortable trading a financial instrument that is more predictable and slower moving you shouldn't trade things like commodities. This trading personality tends to also like less volatility and staying in trades longer. You may want to look at trading Bonds, or slower moving ETF's or stocks. The same holds true for the opposite. If you like trading more volatile and faster moving financial instruments you shouldn't trade Bonds. You should consider higher volatility and faster moving ETF's, stocks or commodities. What happens when you are not trading financial instruments that match your trading personality is you are encouraged by your emotions to get out of trades at the wrong time and not follow your system. An example is, a trader that likes fast moving trades that is in a Bond trade may get bored with the trade. Then not know how to react to these emotions and get out of the trade right before there is finally some price movement. A trader that likes slower moving trades that is in a commodity like Soy and gets nervous because of the high volatility when there a big move against their trade and gets out at the low right before another big move. This time in their direction. Or worst yet, since they like to stay in trades longer they do not get out at their stop and price continues to go against them.

We offer an indicator to our members that shows price movement over a period of time. You may want to consider using this indicator to help you determine what symbols are a better fit with your trading style.

The sooner you realize that you are going to have losing trades and losing periods of time, and then can look at the overall performance of your trading system you will start to build confidence. Think of it like this. If you have a 2:1 RRR, Risk Reward Ratio, you can quickly see that even with a 50% winning ratio you still have a very profitable trading system. Yes, if you are an engineer Risk Reward Ratio may sound backwards to you. The reason we say it this way is that is no reward until you are willing to put up a known amount of risk.

We also recommend that all traders develop a trading plan and follow your plan. You should also have a Trade Log where you log every trade and add comments on why you took the trade. This allows to you go back and see if there are any patterns. This can also be a tool to refine your trading plan. These two documents should become your trading bible.

Using these tools will help you keep fear and the little demons out of your trades, and will help you learn how to react correctly to your emotions.

CHAPTER 11

Master the Art of Trading

How successful traders learn to trade

One way is to find a successful trader and have him teach you exactly how he does it. However, even if you find this person and if he were willing to show you what he does, it would not necessarily make you a successful trader. You might not have the capital necessary to trade the way he does; you definitely do not have the years of experience he spent developing his successful approach Or you might not have the characteristics necessary to be successful with that style of trading.

Another way to learn is by trial and error. This is the method most people use. But with trial and error, you don't always take a loss when you trade incorrectly and you don't always make a profit when you trade correctly, so **many people learn the wrong lesson**. Since some of the best methods generate losses more than half the time, you can take many losses in row applying a very effective system. And, if you have a run of good luck, you can make tons of money trading stupidly. Psychologists label it random reinforcement, and it makes it almost impossible to learn to be a good trader through trial and error.

The most obvious and easiest way is to read books. Find the best books by the most respected authors and the best traders and learn from them. While this may work in other areas of life, it is more problematic for trading.

One of the few real secrets in trading is that most of what you read in books about how to trade does not work in the real world. Even books by respected authors are full of trading methods that lose money when put to the test. You may find this shocking, but almost no trading authors demonstrate the effectiveness of the methods they advocate. The best you can hope for are some well-chosen examples or a few cursory tests. That is why I have two full time programmers on staff. We use Trade Station and computers to back test our systems (without over optimization) to statistically prove our systems. You can download the performance of our core 10 minute per night system at www.howtotradebonus.com.

"It is not enough to have knowledge, one must also apply it." Learning to trade is a combination of being exposed to ideas while gaining practical experience watching the markets on a day-to-day basis. This is not something you can master in only a few weeks. On the plus side, you can become a great trader with only average intelligence if you're persistent. Professional traders describe the makeup of a successful trader like this:

> *"Intelligence alone does not make a great trader. Success is equal parts of intellect, applied psychology, practice, discipline, bankroll, self-understanding and emotional control."*

Moreover, to be successful you don't have to invent some complex approach that only a rocket scientist could understand. Successful trading plans tend to be simple. They follow the general principles of correct trading in a somewhat unique way.

The three phases of a trader's edification

Most new or aspiring traders first start looking around to find a trading system that's guaranteed and never fails. Many spend thousands of dollars on books, seminars and programs before they realize that that no one-size-fits-all system exists.

So, after wasting a fair amount of time and money, they begin to understand that money management, a topic all serious trading teachers cover first, before a single live trade is made, really is required. So they begin risking only a small percentage of their account on any one trade. Instead of placing large bets on a few trades, they experiment with smaller positions.

Finally, they begin to understand that trading psychology really separates the winners from the losers long-term. They try to become aware of their subconscious reactions and emotions as well as those of the market or crowd.

It would be better to begin at phase three and work backward because, as I've said before, the first step in becoming a consistently successful trader is to understand how psychology plays out in your own head and in the way the crowd reacts to changes in the markets. As a trader you'll come to realize that once you make a trade, logic no longer applies because the fear of losing money and greed for more money rear their ugly heads.

But once aspiring traders understand this psychology, they understand why it's important to have a methodology and, more importantly, the discipline to follow it. New traders must realize that once they join a crowd, they lose their individuality and, even worse, crowd psychology impairs their judgment. Because crowds are wrong more often than not - typically selling at market bottoms and buying at market tops.

After the would-be traders understand a bit of psychology, they can focus on money management. Money management is an important subject and deserves much more than just a few sentences. But there are two issues that are critical: (1) risk in terms of any individual trade and (2) risk as a percentage of the trader's overall account.

Now, would be a good time to go register for our free training videos which includes "Trading Psychology Tips" and you can download your free advanced money management software at www.howtotradebonus.com.

After traders understand at least the importance, if not the specific applications, of psychology and money management, then they're better able to find a methodology that suits them and their situation. Keep in mind that there are many ways to muddy the waters, and computerized instant information just makes it that much murkier for the new trader. Don't look for the system with the most complicated charts and graphs; look for one that is simple and easy to understand. It's got a much better chance of working because you'll be much more likely to implement it.

Before You Start Trading Real Money

The first component of your trading plan is the amount of capital you intend to invest. There is a direct relationship between the amount of capital you commit and your probability of success. The more you invest, the greater the likelihood that you will make money.

Most professionals say it takes about $10,000 to start off but I have successfully taught people who had only $5,000 by using very disciplined money management techniques. If you try to trade with less, you won't have the capital necessary to apply proper risk management principles.

An important element when deciding how much to commit initially to trading is that whatever you start with must be money you can afford to lose without affecting your standard of living. It should be money that you feel comfortable putting at risk, the same as if you were making an investment in a new business. Many businesses fail, that's just life. Most start-ups also require additional capital infusions to achieve their maximum potential. If you are afraid of losing your trading money it will affect your ability to make sound trading decisions.

Your Trading Strategy

The next part of your trading plan involves how you will make your actual buying and selling decisions. Under what conditions will you enter trades? When will you exit your trades? What markets will you trade?

There are a few cardinal principles which should be part of every trading strategy:

1) Trade with the trend,

2) Cut losses short,

3) Let profits run,

4) Manage risk

5) Adhere to your plan.

These elements are so basic and important that I have devoted an entire chapter to trading strategy. You must make sure your strategy includes each of these requirements for a successful trading career, and **you must stick to the plan instead of allowing your emotions to dictate your trades**.

But for now, just realize that **a trader without a strategy is his own worst enemy** – particularly when it comes to making money in the markets. He's either too greedy and hangs on too long, sometimes watching a big winner turn into a big loser... or too fearful and settles for a tiny profit, completely missing out on a big winner.

A great trade consists of a great buy and a great sell.

So you must know... what is your exit strategy for the trade? You don't have one? You're not alone; most investors have no exit plan. But if you don't have a plan for when you'll sell, chances are great you'll make an emotional decision and sell at exactly the wrong time.

CHAPTER 12

Money, Money, Money Management

I cannot stress enough how important having and following a proven money management system is to traders of any kind. Every trader and every system will have losses and draw-downs of the account. Some of the most successful traders experience multiple years of negative returns but, because of proper money management, they're able to offset those losing periods with gains that make them overall (big) winners.

The ability to remain in the trading game is key to your long-term success. To be there when the big winners come in, you must vigilantly guard your account balance by limiting your exposure to any one position and by quickly exiting losing trades.

Sounds easy, doesn't it? But, unless you have the discipline to follow a system you have confidence in, you're likely to find yourself holding on to losers, waiting for them to rebound. That's why we train our students to do their trading while the markets are closed and to have their entry and exit points clearly defined before they start a trade. Remember with our system, in no time you will be setting up your trades in only 10 minutes a night.

Take a look at what kind of returns are required just to offset drawdowns:

With a $100,000 account, if you drawdown 10 percent, to $90,000 you'll need to make 11.1 percent to break even.

With a 20 percent drawdown, you'll start at $80,000 and need a 25 percent gain to get it back.

At 25 percent down, you'll need to make 33.3 percent, and with a 30 percent you need to make 42.9 percent to recover.

You can see why, if we assume that at some point any system will suffer 10 consecutive drawdowns, we want to keep each one to a maximum of 2 percent of the trading account. Bumping it up to even 2.5 percent means it takes 72 percent higher profits to make up the losses.

In addition to making it harder to return to the black, the psychological toll of accelerating losses forces many traders out of the game before the winners appear. The key to long term profits is minimizing your risk while being in position when the rewards materialize.

CHAPTER 13
Risky Business

Mastering the Risks and Rewards in Trading

Not mastering risk and reward in trading is probably the main reason why so many traders and investors are destined to fail. It's really dumb when you think about it, because reward/risk is the easiest way to get a definable edge on the market.

The reward/risk equation builds a safety net around your open positions. It's designed to tell you how much can be won, or lost, on each trade you take. The secondary purpose is to remove emotion so you can focus squarely on the numbers.

Let's look at some ways that reward/risk will improve your trading performance.

Every trading opportunity has a directional probability based on a specific pattern. Always execute positions in the highest-odds direction and exit any trades that fail to respond according to your expectations.

Trade positions with the highest reward target to risk target ratios.

Markets move in trend and countertrend waves. Many traders panic during countertrends and exit good positions out of fear. After every trend in your favor, decide how much you're willing to risk when things turn against you. Back up and look for past highs and lows your trade must pass through to get to the reward target. Each price level will present an obstacle that must be overcome.

Timing has as much an impact on your trades as price. Choose a holding period based on the distance and use both price and time for stop-loss management. This will allow you to forgo marginal positions and wait for the best opportunities. Prepare to experience long periods of boredom between frantic surges of concentration. Expect to stand aside, wait and watch when the markets have nothing to offer.

Good trade setups come in various shades of gray. Analyze conflicting information and place the trade when your system signals a go. Careful trade selection controls risk better than any stop-loss system so know that waiting for the right opportunity requires as much deliberation as determining an entry or an exit. **Never enter a position without knowing the exit**. Trading is never a buy-and-hold exercise. Define your exit price in advance, and then stick to it when the stock gets there.

Every trader has a different risk tolerance. Follow your natural tendencies rather than chasing the crowd. If you can't sleep at night, you're trading over your head and need to cut your risk. Don't be fooled by beginner's luck. Trading longevity requires strict self-discipline. It's easy to make money for short periods of time. The markets will take back every penny until you develop a sound risk-management plan. Manage risk on both sides of the trade with focus on optimizing entry and exit points.

Information doesn't equal profit. Charts evolve slowly from one setup to the next. In between, they emit noise in which elements of risk and reward conflict with each other. Enter positions at low risk and exit them at high risk. This often parallels to buying at support and selling at resistance, but it can also be used to trade momentum with safety and precision. Look to exit in wild times in order to increase your reward. Wait for price acceleration and feed your position into the hungry hands of other traders just as the price pushes into a high-risk zone.

CHAPTER 14

A Pro's Top Tips for Building Wealth with Trading

Invest or Trade With the Trend

The fastest and most risk free way to make money in the markets is to identify a change of trend in the market as early as possible, take your position, ride the trend, and close your position shortly after the trend reverses.

Any market professional will tell you that it is impossible to buy at the lows and sell at the highs (or sell at the highs and buy at the lows) consistently, but with trend trading, it is often possible to catch 60 to 80 percent of many intermediate term and long term market movements.

But know, trend trading is not a natural or intuitive process. It's long-term, not terribly exciting and is not based on outsmarting the markets.

Cut Your Losses Quickly

In order to keep trading, you must preserve your capital. It is critical you keep the individual losses small in relation to the overall size of your trading capital. If you can keep trading in the direction of the trend, the big profits will come. If you are risking too high a percentage of your trading capital on each trade, you could end up blowing your entire account.

Our money management system ensures I will never lose more than a small percentage of my trading capital in any single trade. This means that even if I have a string of five consecutive losing trades, I still have the vast majority of my trading capital to continue trading. It is imperative that you have a similar system. Without it, you will not last long in the trading game.

With our system we have a proper stop loss mechanism therefore <u>we often capture 70 to 90 percent of most trend moves</u> since we track the trend direction, liquidity, volatility and momentum and automatically adjust to stay with profitable trades as long as possible and make our profits even larger. This leads to the next point:

You Must Let Your Profitable Trades Run

A winning trader stays with profitable trades as long as possible because the trend is likely to continue and make the profits even larger. We can let profits run while still guarding against the possibility that prices will turn around and take away much of your accumulated profits before the trend actually reverses. We use what is called a trailing stop to move your exit point along behind your trade.

The trailing stop-loss will let profits run while still guarding against the possibility that prices will turn around and take away much of your accumulated profits. As long as the trend keeps moving in your favor, you stay in the trade. If the market reverses direction by the amount of the stop-loss, you exit the trade at that point.

Thus you're always protecting your profits and keeping 80 to 90 percent of the accumulated profit on any good trade.

Manage Risk

The most important element of managing risk is keeping your loss per trade to a very small percentage of your trading capital.

Proper risk management ensures that a trader can continue to trade in the markets even after a string of losing trades (drawdowns). In fact, if you follow a proper risk management strategy you can continue trading or investing in the markets for as long as you live without worrying about losing your entire trading capital. This is what I call "Staying in the Game".

Cut Your Expenses

By using ETFs instead of Mutual Funds, you'll automatically reduce fund management fees to the bare minimum. If you trade individual stocks, options or currencies, you'll incur no management fees. And by learning how to properly place your own buy and sell orders you'll be able to trade for the lowest brokerage fees. Check the various online brokerages and pick the one with the best services and lowest fees.

Remember, short-term trading profits are taxable income. I want you paying more taxes (because your income is rising), but be sure you keep accurate records of all your trading expenses and use them to offset your income. Hiring a tax professional who knows financial market trading can end up saving you more in taxes than they cost. Make all your estimated tax payments on-time and have documentation. Nothing ruins what you thought was a good trading year like an unexpected tax bill from the IRS.

CHAPTER 15

Why Be a Trend Follower

So, if trend trading is unnatural, why exactly do I endorse it so enthusiastically? Basically because it's the easiest, fastest way for an individual with a modest amount of investment capital to make a lot of money over both the short and long term.

If you're a trust fund baby you can let daddy's Wall Street guys worry about it, they've got a direct interest in keeping your account active and producing income for you and them (they're probably using a trend trading system too). But if you've worked and saved your way into a small nest egg and you want to ramp up the growth of and secure your family's financial future, learning to trend trade the financial markets is the ticket.

First off, you'll profit in any kind of market

We don't care whether the bulls or the bears are running the show, there's always a trend we can trade. We really don't care if the trend is a boom or a bust, how long it's been running or why. We just ride the momentum and stash the profits in our accounts.

No More Buy and Hold, Crazy Jim Cramer or CNBC

Trend following decision-making doesn't involve discretion, guesses, "gut" feels or hunches. It's not buy and hold (and pray). It doesn't involve passive indexing or fundamental analysis. No more 24-hour news cycles, daily turbulence or sensational hype. No black boxes or magic formulas either. We can let go of the quest for the Holy Grail. And, with proper preparation, anyone can learn trend trading.

No More Crystal Ball Gazing

Trends are all around us, always coming and always going. We just want to find them and ride them as far as they go. Markets trend up and down too and no one can predict a market trend, you can only react to them. Trend following never anticipates the beginning or end of a trend, it only acts when the trend changes. There is no need to figure out why a market is trending — just follow it. Like you don't need to understand electricity to use it.

Profits In the Center of The Perfect Storm

Trend trading works to compound absolute returns, not to be just like the average investor. The goal is to make the big returns, not generate passbook savings returns. Trend following also has the unique ability to wait for targets of opportunity or outlier events like the 2008 market crash and can make you huge money in those times.

Sound Risk Management

Trend trading has well defined exit protocols to control losses to your account. Using stops and limit orders and proper leverage, trend trading also has low correlation with many other investments. It eliminates exposure to group think and toxic assets allowing you to hedge and actually increase your profit potential. Trend following offers the best protection when bubbles burst and everyone else starts running for shelter.

The Madness of Crowds Works To Your Advantage

It's been said that the markets, which are always changing, are only our subjective expectations reflected objectively. Interestingly, people's reactions to change remains consistent and they almost always bet wrong as a group. Trend following takes advantage of this herd mentality to make money. The strict discipline of the system minimizes behavioral predisposition and resolves our eagerness to realize gains and reluctance to realize losses. Most peoples' behaviors are driven by impulsive instead of purposeful choices. Trend trading wins because we recognize and use our knowledge of trends.

It's The Modern, Scientific Way to Trade

Trend trading doesn't require a belief; it relies on principles proven over decades. It has a defined edge (a lot like the MIT card counting team that beat the Vegas casinos chronicled in the movie "21"). With trend trading you learn to be the casino and not the losing blackjack player. You use rules rooted in numbers, based on process not outcomes. And remember, your frequency of correctness does not matter; only the magnitude matters. Who cares about your winning percentage? It means nothing. The only belief you need is your consistent confidence in a proven trend trading system. Our low risk trend trading system has proven to be robust in its consistent performance year after year.

To learn more about our Low Risk Trend Trading system go register for our free training videos at *www.howtotradebonus.com*.

Allows You to Profit Without Devoting Your Life to Charts and Ticks

How much time will trend trading take? You won't be stuck staring at the computer screen drinking coffee and ignoring your family and health. Once you are set up, 10 minutes a day is all you need when you approach trading like an engineer.

Performs Like a Champ in Crisis Periods

Trend trading is adaptable and performs best during periods of rising volatility and uncertainty. You can count on it: The unknown will happen again. Every boom will bust, disasters, natural and man-made, will happen. Are you ready? You have to be able to ride the waves while riding out the storm, and trend trading allows you to be in the right place at the right time.

Trend Trading Does Not Discriminate

It's not restricted to any single market or instrument. Our focus on price action allows us to apply it to a large variety of markets because price is the one thing that all markets have in common. That means a system for treasury bonds will work on the Euro, too. And if you switch it over to coffee, the principles still work. Trend following is robust, but you have to trust your buy and sell signals and follow your rules.

No Bailouts Needed for Trend Traders

Forget Social Security, bailouts, stimulus plans, and roads to nowhere. Those won't help you to make money, but they will cost you (as a taxpayer) money. No matter which way the fiscal system veers, if your system is grounded in sound principles you win, and the government has almost no say in your success.

But We Must Remember

The market does not care about you or know you. It doesn't care about your dreams or desires. It is the ultimate authority so you better listen to it.

A few basic rules to keep in mind as you begin to trend trade:

It is imperative that you identify and trade with the trend. This is the primary tenet of trend trading; do not violate this rule. Stick with the trend until the trend reverses.

Learn to identify reverses and not be fooled by pull-backs. Recognizing and then staying with the trend is the most important part of this strategy. Since things in motion usually stay in motion, don't fight it; let it continue along its trajectory and trade with it. Never short a rising market and do not buy a down market.

Accept the fact that you are almost never going to sell precisely at the top or buy at the bottom. Still, when you detect the start of a trend you'll get in early enough to generate a lot of profits. So save yourself the agony of attempting to predict the tops or bottoms; tops and bottoms are only identifiable after they have been made. Trying to predict them is usually a losing proposition, but learning to identify and profit from trends will make you wealthy.

Just what is a trend, for trading purposes?

When we say trend trading, we're talking about the general direction (up, down, sideways) of the price of a particular asset or the markets in general. Trend trading can be applied to the equities markets, the debt (bond) markets, the commodities markets, even the collectibles markets. Each market has its own signals and strategies for identifying and profiting from trends. Once you learn to trade one market, you can branch out into others.

Trend trading is one of the easiest and most effective ways for making money in these markets. It depends on identifying and acting on a trend near its beginning and getting out once it reverses.

Trend traders take a position in a market and often hold it for weeks or even months and reap large gains in the process. By trading longer term (secular) trends, we're able to discount day-to-day volatility and concentrate on the bigger picture. **Trend trading is considered one of the easiest yet low risk ways to make money in the financial markets**. With our trend trading system and by following the simple rules associated with the signals, you can expect to catch 60 to 80 percent of intermediate and long-term movements, without having to watch the markets constantly.

But just because it's easy to conceptualize doesn't mean it's easy to implement. The positions and trades successful trend traders make are often counter to both emotions and the prevailing wisdom. "Buy low, sell high" is the mantra of making money in the financial markets, but how do we know when it's low enough to buy? According to Wall Street legend, the mantra that says the time to buy is when there is "blood in the streets."

The maxim has been attributed to financier Bernard Baruch in the early 20th century and to industrialist John D. Rockefeller, Sr., but it's most frequently attributed to Baron Rothschild. During the Panic of 1871 in Paris, as Napoleon was being defeated and captured by the Germans and the working class was revolting, blood was literally running in the streets. The landed gentry sold off their Paris property in a panic allowing Baron Rothschild (according to the story) to buy real estate for centimes (pennies) on the franc.

Conversely, trend traders must avoid getting swept up in bubbles and allowing their greed to override the sell (or short) signal their system sends. There's also the issue of our reluctance to admit failure (cut your losers) and our attachment to a particular investment overriding the rational decision to buy or sell a particular equity or debt instrument. As mentioned earlier taming the ego and emotions is not always so easy. That is why we have included some valuable "Trading Psychology Tips" to help you in your bonus section at *www.howtotradebonus.com*.

But, before we get into psychology, let's define a few terms traders use:

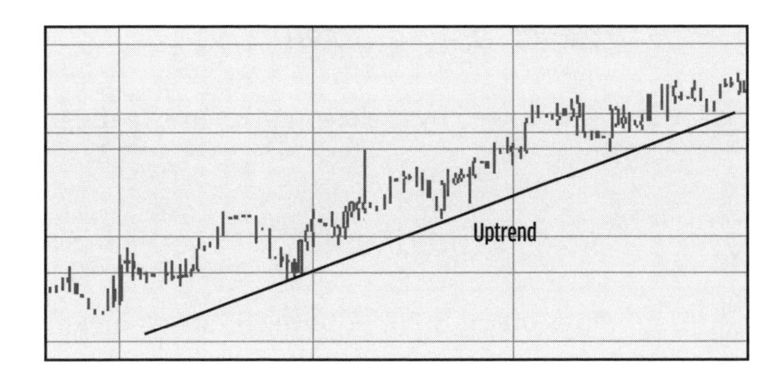

Upward Trend

As the chart below demonstrates, the closing prices, whether higher or lower than the previous day, show consistently higher highs and lows that are higher than previous lows.

Downward Trend

The next chart shows an example of prices that are trending lower. It is characterized by closing highs that are lower than previous highs and lows that are lower.

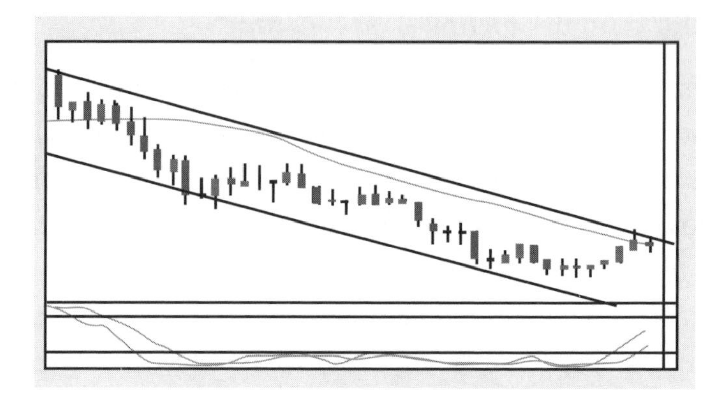

Reversal to an uptrend

This pattern has a higher high followed by a closing price below the previous low.

Reversal to a downtrend

Shows a lower low followed by a closing price above the previous high.

Breakout

When a stock breaks out, it breaks above what was previously a ceiling for it. At that point, it has no ceiling above it as resistance. The longer it takes to break through a ceiling, and the more attempts it makes, usually signifies a stronger support on the downside.

Chartists have dozens of names for patterns and, as you've probably guessed, the period of time the chart covers has a great deal to do with the pattern you see.

But remember, trend traders seek to trade where the momentum is going and to limit losses while letting the winners run.

Most of us, on instinct, want to buy when things are cheap and getting cheaper. So there is a normal temptation to purchase a stock or other asset when it's declining in value because it is getting cheaper. However, the allure of averaging down has bankrupted many traders and investors. Trend traders sell when prices are in decline (shorting) until a reversal is detected. Falling equity prices usually continue downward well past anyone's ability to imagine and rising asset prices typically continue past a ceiling.

Why the trend really is your friend.

As a small fry in the big trading pond, you're not in charge. Your ability to identify what the big players or market is doing and follow their lead is what trend trading is all about. Successful traders don't make things happen or try and predict the future based on fundamentals. Instead, they pay attention to what's happening and follow their system's signals.

The observation of trend isn't a new idea, it's just so much easier now with computer generated charts and access to information. Charles Dow, the author of the Dow Theory observed, at the beginning of the 20th century, that the markets have three trends:

- Long Term, measured in years,
- Intermediate, measured in months, and
- Short-Term over days or weeks.

Another famous market technician, Robert Rhea, called them Tides, Waves and Ripples. He taught us to trade with the tide and use the waves and ripples to time our entries and exits.

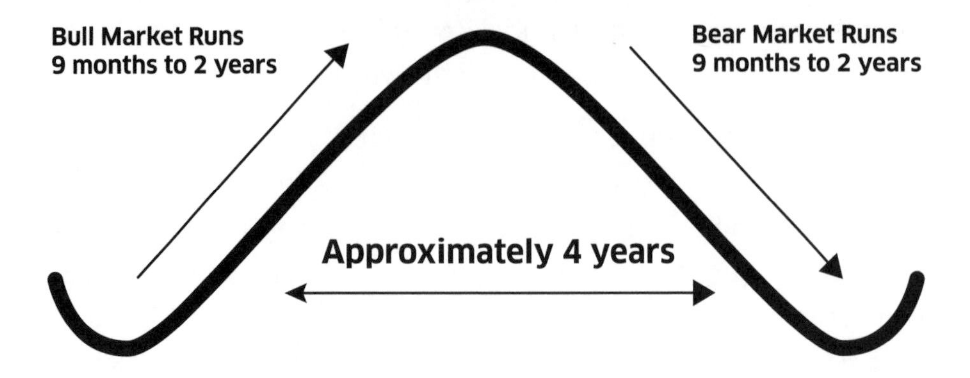

Support and resistance, or trend lines, will tell you what's going on in the market. Instead of focusing on the noise of the hourly and daily fluctuations in prices, you want to ride the longer term movements. Those same trend lines indicate where to place stops and limits to protect our portfolios from significant losses while allowing us to hold on to our winners.

You create wealth by identifying changes in trends, riding the trend and taking your profits at the end of the trend. You can do this in up-trending Bull markets and down-trending Bear markets with the right system.

For those in long positions (buy low, sell high), this chart illustrates when trend selling is the most profitable.

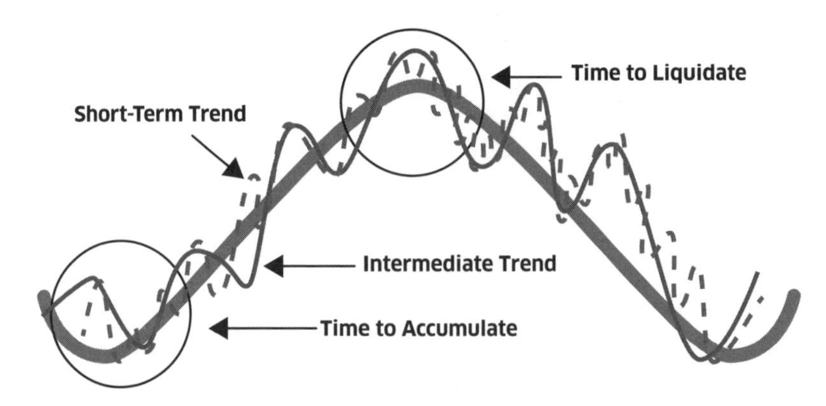

Many markets spend 60 to 75 percent of the time within trading ranges where the opportunity to make profitable trades is slim. So identifying and taking advantage of the trends during the 25 to 40 percent of the time a market is trending is critical to making trading profits. It's easy to see trends in historical charts, harder to spot them as they form. That's why you must use a system and follow its signals.

The death of Buy, Hold and Pray (BHP)

Let's concede that buy and hold may have been a good investment strategy in the past. Wealthy folks bought equity in companies that returned part of the profits as dividends and increased the value of the company by investing the rest of the earnings in growing the business. That era ended several decades ago. Many investors want to hang on to the Middle Ages philosophy that said there was a fair price that goods and services should sell for instead of the modern, market based reality that tells us any price agreed to by a buyer and a seller is fair – supply and demand determine price.

The financial markets have become more casino-like and those who don't acknowledge that the game has changed have a vested interest in ignoring reality or getting the average investor/saver to buy into the illusion. Buy and hold has not worked in at least 10 years and those that promote it don't actually practice it. They want you to buy shares in their Mutual Funds and hold them while they trade the fund's holdings, often buying high and selling low to window-dress the quarterly statements and generating brokerage fees for their sister companies.

Emotional control and traders

How well do you deal with uncertainty? If you're typical, you have a strong need to be right. This need causes amateur traders to hold on to losers waiting for them to turn-around. Professionals get out of losing positions fast, cutting their losses with little emotion, and move on to the next opportunity. Many successful traders are wrong more often than they're right, but the winning trades pay off in excess of the losses.

Having a system and following its signals makes removing emotions easier for all traders but is critical for new traders.

Greed and fear stalk traders

Yes, even experienced professional traders must fight the two biggies: greed and fear. Greed tempts us to hold out for bigger gains even when our signals say get out, fear comes calling when we see red in the P&L column. Conquering greed and fear doesn't mean you'll quit feeling the emotions, it means you quit acting on them.

Feeling guilt and fear over a trading loss isn't irrational. Fear is part of what's made us so successful as a species. It's driven us to build systems to protect ourselves and our families. So when you lose money, you fear for your survival. And, as a trader, if you don't have a system in place to deal with the risks, your fear of loss is justified.

But understanding your emotions and acting on them are two very different things. As a trader you acknowledge the feeling and take the prescribed action in spite of the fear.

But you can only do this if you are confident you have a system that minimizes your risks and allows you to be successful over the long haul. This is where your money management system is invaluable. **You can go register for our free advanced money management software at *www.howtotradebonus.com.***

Running Scared leads to blow-ups

The inability to control fear is what causes traders to bet-the-farm on any one trade looking to make-up for previous losses. Without proper money management, new traders find themselves with huge drawdowns that no trading account can survive.

Knowing your portfolio can survive even 10 drawdowns in succession allows you to continue to trade and be in the market when the inevitable winners come along. By treating your trading as a business, with funds separated from your living expenses, you'll be able to adapt and view both your winners and losers more objectively.

Nerves of Steel vs. a Workable Plan

Many people believe traders must be robots who have walled off their human emotions. But, with the possible exceptions of Vulcans (Mr. Spock joke), I've never met a self-conscious being without emotions. What successful traders have is a system, a plan. This arrangement allows us to look at every possible outcome and decide ahead of time what our reaction will be.

There's always a trend to trade

Even though the broad market spends much of the time in holding patterns, within sectors there is always a trend we can identify and trade on. For those who learn to go short (sell high, buy low) as well as go long (buy low, sell high), the opportunity to take trading profits is almost unending. **This makes trend trading the "Perfect Business"**. The market is always moving and there is always a trend of opportunity to take profit.

This also means you shouldn't worry about taking time off and being out of the markets. It's much easier to enjoy a vacation or visiting loved ones when you don't feel like you have to check in with the markets every day. When you return you'll be able to identify a trend in some sector and pick-up your trading refreshed and with a new enthusiasm.

It's an aggressive trader's delight

For the trader who likes to trade heavily, using the highest possible leverage trend trading allows them (with the right plan) to experience some significantly larger profits. They must also be willing to accept that their trading account drawdowns will be larger during a losing streak. As your trading account expands, you can chose to use a portion of it to make the most aggressive trades using a trend trading system.

And, a conservative traders' salvation

Trend trading also allows the more risk adverse to participate in the upside without accepting heavy losses when the trades go against them.

A large amount of your success will be based on your risk management

Both aggressive and conservative traders use the risk management built into a trend trading system to magnify their gains and minimize their losses.

Design your strategy to suit yourself

Trend trading offers the opportunity for an almost unlimited number of strategies. A beginner starts off learning and applying one or two basic approaches and when they've mastered them, there's always more to learn.

As in most cases, timing is everything

Trend trading naturally allows us to time the markets and economic cycles, but there's no crystal ball required. Instead of anticipating moves we simply follow along and profit.

To get help in designing your own strategy and portfolio go register at *www.howtotradebonus.com*. In your bonus section you will be able to view our free training video, "**How to construct a conservative moderate, or aggressive portfolio.**"

CHAPTER 16

Trading Strategy: Your Key To Success

Your trading strategy is a set of predefined rules for making your buy and sell decisions. Having, and faithfully using, a strategy allows you to make better decisions and control the emotional facet of trading.

For a strategy to work, it must be a set of rules you do not deviate from that dictate how you respond to market moves.

Historical trading data and back testing of the system with the data will allow you develop confidence in the system. Further testing in the current market via virtual trading allows the trader to become comfortable with using the decision making parameters and executing the system's signed trades.

Many elements go into developing a successful trading system including: returns, risk, volatility, timeframe, style, the characteristics of the particular market, and the capital required to operate the system. During your test period, you'll be able to evaluate the system's strategy and how it fits into your style and circumstances. If you only have $10,000 to start, a system that requires $100,000 won't work for you.

All trend trading systems rely on the following basic premises.

Go With the Trend

There's always a trend to trade so you must understand how the system works in relation to a time frame. When you determine the trend, it will be the two-week trend or the six-month trend or the hourly trend. So it's an important part of the trading plan to decide what time frame to use for making decisions.

There are long-term or position traders who hold positions for weeks or months.

Then we have the short-term traders who hold positions for only a few days.

And there are very short-term or day traders who watch the markets all day and always enter and exit their positions on the same day. They take many small profits that (hopefully) add up to larger gains.

Day trading is attractive because you start each day fresh and sleep comfortably at night since you have no open positions. However, it is the most difficult kind of trading there is for most people because it requires total discipline and focus. Trader Larry Williams says:

> *"Day trading is so stressful. You're going to end up frying your brain. All the day traders I talk with are losing money. Besides, it's really hard to come up with profitable day trading systems."*

While it may be easier psychologically to keep the time frame short, **the best results (and a better lifestyle) come from longer-term trading**. The stress notwithstanding, there are some successful long-time day traders, but they're a unique breed. Most didn't start their trading careers as day traders, they built up to it.

For a better chance of success as a new trader, your time frame for trends should be measured in weeks; you enter trades in the direction of the price trend for the last x number of weeks or more. An example of a trend-following entry rule would be to buy whenever today's closing price is higher than the closing price of 25 market days ago, and sell whenever today's closing price is lower than the closing price of 25 market days ago.

When you trade in the direction of a long trend, you are following the markets rather than trying to predict them. Most unsuccessful traders spend their entire (often short) careers looking for ways to predict the markets rather than just following the money.

Cut Your Losers Quickly, Let Your Profits Run

You're going to have losing trades – many profitable systems have more losers than winners. The reason they're profitable is because the losing trade are kept small and the winning trades are allowed to inflate or run.

It sounds easy but in practice many traders find it difficult to admit that the trade they entered has not performed the way they expected. Rather than wait (hope and pray) that it recovers they need to sell, realize a small loss and move on to the next trade. This is hard to do because most of us hate to admit failure.

We were raised in a system that rewarded degrees of success (A– D) and punished failure (F). Those who can reform their idea of failure to be a sign of a learning experience will find cutting losers short easier. Maybe remembering what Edison said when asked about his over 1,000 attempts to produce an incandescent light bulb: "We now know a thousand ways not to build a light bulb".

Letting profits run can be just as challenging. There's even a widely quoted Wall Street quip that says no one ever went broke taking a profit but truthfully, there are many examples of traders who lacked the discipline to stay with a profitable trade during the last of the uptrend or who did not take their profits when their system indicated it was time.

If a trader holds a position that reaches the planned profit level and cancels his sell order trying to capture even more, he risks settling for less or even a loss if the trend turns and he misses the opportunity to sell because he gambled on it surpassing the peak or valley. This is where the saying *pigs get fat, hogs get slaughtered* comes from.

Discipline and confidence in the system allow traders to profit in spite of their fear and greed. A very large amount of a profitable trader's success comes from sticking to the system and executing the indicated trades.

To be a system, it must provide both entry and exit points for winning and losing trades. A written plan, developed before the trade is executed, will increase your success rate exponentially. A daily review, referencing the plan and the performance of the market and the trade, will allow you to quickly cut the losers and stay with the winners.

Believe me, it's easy to read this and say to yourself "Yeah, I can dump those losers fast and hang on to the winners." But unless you have a clearly defined plan and a system that helps you set exit points, you're likely to find yourself (like the majority of novice traders) banking the small gains of your winners and letting your losses pile up while you wait for them to rebound.

Risk Management

Risk management is synonymous with money management for traders. And the question your risk management system must address is: When you make a trade, how much do you trade?

In an article titled *Managing Your Money*, Gibbons Burke, Editor of MarketHistory.com at Morningstar starts off by noting:

> *"Money management is like sex: Everyone does it, one way or another, but not many like to talk about it and some do it*

better than others. But there's a big difference: Sex sites on the Web proliferate, while sites devoted to the art and science of money management are somewhat difficult to find."

Without a sound risk- and money- management system in place, before you ever make one live trade, I am convinced you will never become a successful trader.

Exactly how much of your trading account you risk on any one trade is dictated by your risk tolerance and your balance, but to execute a trade without knowing exactly how much you're risking is asking to have your trade account taken away from you by the smart traders. You must limit the amount you're willing to lose on every trade. Contingent on making a trade you must decide how many units to buy or sell. **Risk management allows you to make a knowledgeable, logical decision on the amount of risk you take on with any trade**.

There's risk with both trading too little and too much. If you don't risk enough, your returns will suffer and you may decide that even if your trading is profitable, the time, expenses and investment required aren't worth the small reward. This is called under trading. You increase your rewards by increasing your risk, but you must realize this also increases the size of your drawdowns. Eventually you can increase the risk to the point of overtrading where the potential for having your entire trading account wiped out by one drawdown is extreme.

You must find the level of risk that produces a sufficient reward, but where you can still handle the drawdown. You must always:

- Know how much you are willing to risk on any one trade
- Understand the risk of the trade and size it to fit your risk tolerance

- Track your trade and pay attention to the risk
- Take your small losses
- Honestly review your actions and be willing to make corrections

You must determine the risk of any one trade, before you enter it. This requires that your plan include a specific exit point. It really doesn't matter how you decide what price you will exit a losing trade at, use a ouija board, consult the stars, or read the charts. What matters is that you have an exit strategy and you know exactly what you will do ahead of time so you can act counter-intuitively, take the small loss and move on. You must always have an exit strategy.

Because I (and every real professional trader you encounter) feel so strongly about this issue, I give away, to anyone who joins me for a short trading presentation via a monthly webinar, a money management spreadsheet. If you'd rather, you can do the calculations yourself.

The formula is **s = e*r/p-x**.

> S equals the size of the trade, e is your portfolio equity and r is the maximum percentage of your portfolio you want to risk on any one trade (I recommend using two percent). P is your entry price and x is your exit price or stop loss.
>
> For example: with an account of $100,000 and a two percent risk factor, you are willing to risk a $2,000 loss on any one trade. If you buy a stock (or ETF) for $100 with a reversal point at $95, the formula says to buy 400 shares. To enter the position will take $40,000 of your funds but with a stop loss at $95 you risk losing only $2,000.
>
> Remember, you only want to risk two percent, no matter what the value of your account. If the stock in our example goes to $120 and the stop is left at $95, the risk increases to nine

percent. Many people consider their profits "house money" and get sloppy about controlling the risk with a winning trade. But, if you want to be a long-time trader with a profitable account, you need to maintain discipline and risk management is critical.

Check free coupon on the back of this book for detailed information on your next opportunity to listen in on our free webinar and get your free money management worksheet with the calculations already pre-programmed for you or visit *www.howtotradebonus.com*.

CHAPTER 17

How to pick a trend trading system

As you look at the systems available, you're going to want to answer as many of these questions as possible. With historical data and easy to use charting software available at nominal cost, you can run as many tests and back tests as you need to be certain the system you're considering works.

- What are the largest (actual and simulated) drawdowns traders using this system have experienced?
- What was the maximum loss in a single trade?
- Look at the worst case scenario, not the rosy picture the salesman paints you. Use historical data and be honest. Would you, could you, stomach the maximum losses individually or cumulatively?
- What is the maximum number of consecutive losing trades this system has sustained?
- All systems go through periods of loss, but knowing what to expect in the worst case will help you make the proper choice.
- How often do draw-downs occur?
- Are the draw-downs quick or do they develop gradually?

- All trading systems experience losing trades. Many have more losers than winners but are profitable overall because the losers are cut short and the reduction to the portfolio or drawdown, is controlled by money management. Being aware of what to expect allows the new trader to accept the losers as part of the process.

- On average, how long does it take to recover the losses incurred in an average draw-down?

- What's the longest time to recovery from the bottom of a draw-down?

- Is the risk of each trade quantified? What variables are used to calculate the risk?

- How is overall risk controlled? I've just explained how to calculate the risk and how important it is. Look carefully at what your system says and does about risk.

- Are there any circumstances when trading could be halted to avoid further losses? If so, what are they; if not, why not?

- Are there markets where the trading system performs poorly? If so, why?

- Does the system adapt quickly or slowly to changes in market volatility?

- Does the system have a way to minimize losses caused by whipsaws (sudden unexpected volatility) in the market?

- Does the system include periods where it remains on the sidelines and then calls for resuming trading when certain market conditions warrant it? If so, what are those periods and conditions?

- How are stops chosen and placed?
- What kind of role does portfolio diversification play in risk reduction?

Of the thousands of new and experienced traders we have surveyed over the years, over 75% did not consider the above questions in making their decision as to what trading system was right for them. Answering these questions will help you from making poorly conceived, spontaneous, thoughtless, and emotional based decisions. The result for not doing your due diligence is loss of time and lots of money.

I would suggest you not only ask the questions but also try to understanding the why of the questions. **To gain a better understanding as to the why of these important decision making questions I would suggest to download our statistical performance record at *www.howtotradebonus.com***

CHAPTER 18

Components of a Trend Trading System

A word of warning: Once you spend a little time in the trading and investing world you'll realize there are many more people making money selling systems than there are people who actually make money trading the systems they sell. Many people who are famous traders are really famous salesmen of trading systems. Most of the so called experts don't trade for themselves or clients; they sell books, CDs/DVDs and workshops about trading.

Before buying a course or following a system, investigate the seller. Find out what kind of reputation he has and what previous buyers' experiences are. You'll also want to be clear about what markets you will be trading in. Trend trading can work in any market that produces a daily price chart. Most brokerages handle stocks and ETFs, but investigate your options if you're considering commodities or currencies for trading since not all brokers deal in those markets. You'll also want to compare prices. Active traders usually get a reduced rate per trade. If you don't see a discount for volume, ask for one.

Position sizing is critical for controlling risks. Be sure the system you're considering has clear and easy to follow rules regarding the percentage of your trading account to use when you buy or sell.

Your entry and exit points are vitally important. Your system should give you clear prices to buy into (or sell if short) and, even more importantly, the exit points whether it's a winning or a losing trade.

Does the system give clear guidance for using stop orders? These protect your profits and your trading account from large losses.

You'll want clear and relevant tactics to properly execute your orders.

The system we've developed has the following components. I suggest you compare any others you're considering with this to see if it is a complete program.

Quick Start Guide: For the more advanced traders already familiar with ETFs who want to get started quickly.

4 Video DVD's: Contain the foundations of the ETF home study course. You simply put the DVDs into your computer or DVD player and follow the tutorial. We give you lots of examples and show you what each step of the process looks like. You'll develop a fundamental understanding of ETFs (exchange traded funds) by watching my examples, my definitions, and the details of the system.

ETF System Training Manual: Includes many practical examples of ETF trading. You'll be able to see what the charts look like when they produce the signals we look for that indicate entry and exit positions. We include examples to illustrate both profitable and losing trades that bring the ETF system into focus for you.

Email Support: Clients receive unlimited email support for 6 months (or life) after they complete the home study course, live webinars, and visit the FAQ area where many past students' questions have already been answered.

Personal Training: All our clients get 6 months (or lifetime depending what level a new member chooses) mentorship. We only take on a limited number of students periodically so we can answer and new member questions. The owner of ETF Trend Trading and support coaches have over 50 years combined market experience and have traded billions of dollars (with leverage) over the years. If you think you learned a few things in this book, wait until you are a full member.

ETF Course Training: We conduct ongoing training in a webinar format (no cost through your internet connection) for 1-6 hours each week (not counting our live market day trade room for those that are interested in day trading). This allows us to address the current market situations and delve deeper into the signals our system is currently producing. Students also find the discipline of regularly scheduled training helps them progress more rapidly.

Additional Resources: We allow each new student 6 months access to my "Advanced Members Area" where they can follow some of our own personal trades in real time. We also maintain a personal blog where we reveal and discuss our trades. Each day we post the next day's trades with entry points, stops, and limits. We also go into the details behind each of our positions, which helps reinforce the ETF Trend Trading system rules.

Trading Psychology: We discusses in detail the importance for traders, whether they're new or experienced, of following the system rules instead of their emotions, hunches or tips. Their access to our forum and to our professional team of traders allows them to develop confidence in the system and learn from others successes and failures.

Trader's Money Management: Our system has a very detailed set of rules for risk control using a method called position sizing. In addition, students learn the proper set up of technical stops to limit the draw-downs in their trading account. This is an absolutely critical part of a trading program. There must be a money management plan in any kind of professional trading system.

List of ETFs: We compile an exclusive, continually updated proprietary list of the ETFs that are most appropriate for our students to trade. As part of the time management built into our program, we advise students on which funds, out of the thousands now available, to spend their time tracking and trading.

A 24-month Retirement Plan: This special report gives a step-by-step guide to successfully transitioning into a trader's lifestyle, leaving behind the 9-5 job (if you choose). Following this plan helps students keep the end in mind as they learn the system.

PD Trade Scanner Software: This software scans thousands of funds each trading day and helps us find and execute the best ETF trades. By using the software, we limit the amount of time you must spend to successfully implement the system.

Guarantee: For the serious student who tries my system and finds it's not for them, we offer a 100 percent refund during the first 90 days as long as the buyer has tried the program for a minimum of 30 days trading a live or demo account. That gives all buyers a chance to try it out for three times longer than the usual 30 day refund period we are legally required to offer. We require proof of giving the system a try because we don't want a bunch of impulse buyers who never even open the course after we ship it out. I guarantee you no system no matter how good it is will work for you if it remains in the box on your kitchen table. When I say proof you tried it I mean a simple 30 day broker demo report. You're going to need a demo (paper money account) to have charts so it's not a big deal.

You'd be shocked to know that a small percentage think that money will fall from the sky when they join our mentorship program and they won't even bother to open a brokerage account. This is an easy simple stipulation for those that are serious. If you are presently considering a trading course that has a shorter refund period, be sure you have time to really give it a try before your time runs out.

A FEW MORE QUESTIONS YOU WANT TO ASK BEFORE STARTING A NEW PROGRAM

Is this a system for experienced traders, those with some experience or people brand new to the markets?

Experienced traders can glean a lot of useful information from my system and some buy it just to gain access to my personal trading journal and software (because they'll be able to reduce the time they spend watching the markets each day). But the system starts from the assumption that the student has never traded the markets. We cover where and how to open a brokerage account and how to trade virtually before committing any money to the program. For us it is very enjoyable and rewarding teaching people who have little or no trading experience; they're always so enthusiastic and grateful!

What style of trading does the system follow?

Our ETF Trend Trading System is based on following the trends using technical analysis as its basis. It signals trades in markets that are going up or down, and in consolidating markets, too. By using technical analysis to indicate trading opportunities, we take advantage of the fact that ETFs tend to move in trends 30 percent of the time. So we look to identify the trends and profit on the movement in prices.

How much time does the system require you to spend researching stock selections and reading charts?

One of the unique features of our system is that we use daily bars that enable us to make quick, after-market decisions and **set our trades for the next day in about 5 or 10 minutes per night**. In the "Advanced Members Area" (available free to all new members for the first 90 days) you can find our personal trades with the entry points, stops, and limits that you can mimic. This might take an additional 5 minutes each night.

How much startup capital does the system require?

While I've seen people start with less, we recommend having a $5,000 trading account to start. This allows you to keep the risk for each trade within the systems rules while producing significant profits. If you use our systems on futures or forex you can start with only $2,000.

Is it a day trading system?

Day traders close out all their positions each evening before the markets close. It requires a lot more time that must correspond to the markets' hours (if you're on the west coast of the USA that means working from 6:30 am until 1 pm, for instance, if you're trading the New York markets).

We do cover how to use trend trading for day trading, but that is not required since we look to capitalizes on trends that may last for weeks or months. Even though the system's total non-compounded monthly profit averages 6 percent per month, on any one trade you will only risk 1 to 2 percent of your account (if you're following the money management rules). That's while spending **only 10 minutes per night**, working while the USA markets are closed.

More aggressive traders who want to spend their time day trading the system often average closer to 12 percent profits per month but they're pretty much working it as a full-time business. Still, they choose how many days per month to work, taking holidays whenever they decide instead of a boss telling them when they can take off. And they can work it only part-time if they chose to, though that tends to reduce their earnings. We do have a separate day trading program for those that are interested.

Note: Positive past performance is no guarantee of future performance. Please read the full risk disclaimer on *www.howtotradebonus.com*

CHAPTER 19

The Trend Trader's Golden Rules:

Never Risk More Than You Can Afford To Lose

Your trading account must never include money you need to meet your living expenses. If you choose to take some of your profits to spend or invest in other assets, remove them from the trading account before redeploying them.

In your trading account, you use money management to determine how much to risk on any one trade. I use a unique position sizing method that combines a percentage risk stop and a technical stop price that allows us to increase the returns while maintaining our risk target.

Check free coupon on the back of this book for detailed information on your next opportunity to listen in on our free webinar and get your free money/risk management worksheet with the calculations already pre-programmed for you or visit your bonus section at *www.howtotradebonus.com*.

Don't Let Fear and Greed Sabotage Your Trading

When you base your buying and selling decisions on a trend trading system instead of your emotions, your results become predictably profitable. With a proven system, support from experienced traders and a simple structure with clear buy and sell signals, trading becomes a pleasure instead of a chore. If you take the actions the system indicates, you'll be rewarded with the profits and self-confidence that the pros enjoy.

Don't Let The Insiders Steal From You

Small, individual traders must learn to avoid the traps the big market players lay for them. You can either learn the hard way that the hedge fund managers are hunting your stops or you let someone like me, who's been there and done that, to show you how to avoid the traps.

Remember, Small Trades Equal Big Returns

It's paradoxical but you will be more successful overall if you risk only one or two percent of your account on any one trade. A disciplined trend trading system will allow you to capture a significant portion of profits with your winning trades and minimize your drawdowns from the unprofitable ones. Over the course of your trading career, this combination can make you outsized profits. First, you'll be in the market when those big winners show up, and you'll cut your losers short so you'll have less to make up to get into the plus column.

Trading Isn't a Fair Game

Traders incur costs in addition to gains or losses. Unlike a fair game where winnings and losses are equal, trading is not a zero sum game because of the transaction costs. Like the casinos in Las Vegas and Atlantic City (and more places everyday it seems) where the house always wins because they pay out less than they take in, the financial markets extract fees for playing the game. To be a truly profitable trader requires that your winners out earn your losers by a substantial margin. The only way you have a chance of doing this is to recognize and accept your biases and limitations and use a system designed to overcome them.

You Don't Want to Live the Typical Trader's Lifestyle

Professional traders spend most of their waking hours studying charts and looking for ways to beat their competition. As an individual, part-time trader, you're going to need a system that allows you to identify a trend, enter and exit at appropriate times, and control your risk without spending the majority of your life at the computer.

Our system, that you can follow with as little as ten minutes in the evening after the markets are closed, offers you all the potential rewards of trend trading and minimizes the risks. As a bonus, this allows you to make your trading decisions while the markets are closed, so you'll find it much easier to control your emotions and follow the system's indicators.

Learn from the Legends

Now that we're into the celebrity trader era with CNBC and MSNBC broadcasting non-stop financial news and opinions, who you study and take note of is critical to your success.

I for one would rather be rich than famous and many of the most successful traders feel the same way. Some, like Warren Buffett and Jim Rodgers feel a sense of duty to try to enlighten the masses of new market participants. Others, like me, find they enjoy teaching new traders the ropes and helping average traders match the performance of professional traders.

The best place to start (besides my book and free mini course ☺) is with Jack Schwager's books:

Market Wizards and The New Market Wizards.

By reading about professional traders you'll gain an understanding of what pros really do and think about the markets and find some you can relate to.

I also recommend Trading In the Zone by Mark Douglas

Don't Let Hucksters Scam You

Over the last 20 years, as working class people have been transitioned from defined benefit pensions managed by professionals to defined contribution plans they're responsible for, the professionals have found it easy to extract substantial gains from these untrained traders.

In response to the public's realization that they need to learn to function in the financial markets, Trading Gurus, who've never actually traded professionally, travel the country with slick sales pitches and promises of easy money.

So, while you must learn to actively manage your portfolio and trade the markets, you must guard your money and your time from the scam artists now trolling these parts.

Run; don't walk, from anyone who tells you they can double your money this year (or any year). Ask to see 5 years' worth of trading records. **If it seems too good (and easy) to be true, it is**. A system you don't understand, that simply sends you signals, buy/sell, green/red arrow, isn't going to work over the long term and probably not even the short term.

Use All Your Tools

Today's traders can, for a very modest investment, have more computing and communications tools than the richest, most powerful

Wall Street firms did just 20 years ago. But you've got to learn to use them to your advantage, not become a slave to them. This isn't a detailed training, but all my students are taught exactly how to spend just 10 minutes a day, while the markets are closed, reading the charts and placing their orders.

CHAPTER 20

Frequently Asked Questions about Trading ETFs

1. Are ETFs the Right Investment for Individual Investors?

Yes. The term Exchange Traded Fund or ETF may sound like a fancy financial term, but they're really just a better version of Mutual Funds which were created for non-professional investors. Because ETFs are more transparent and are not actively managed (and so don't have big management fees), a small investor can build a diversified position or trade a sector with a small initial investment. Now that options and electronic trading are universally available, investors wanting to actively trade can also use ETFs to reduce risks (compared to any one individual stock) and enhance their returns.

2. How Much Money Is Required to Start Investing in ETFs?

What does one share, plus transaction fee, cost? Realistically, if you have as little as $1,000 that you're ready to commit for the next few years, you can start buying and selling ETFs. If you think you may need the money to cover emergencies or pay upcoming bills, keep it in a savings account because you'll pay to cash out the ETFs and you may have to sell at a loss to convert an equity investment to cash quickly.

3. Can I Diversify Internationally Using ETFs?

Yes. There are ETFs that are composed of stocks within a sector that include both US and international companies. There are also ETFs that hold only stocks of companies based in one particular country or region of the world. Using ETFs is a much more cost effective way to hold equities in less developed areas where buying and selling on their local exchanges is costly and time consuming.

4. What About Fixed Income Investments, Can ETFs help me?

Yes. There are funds that hold tax-free munis, a great way to reduce your taxes if you're in a high tax bracket; there are Corporate Bond ETFs, US Treasury Bond and TIPS (Treasury Inflation-Protected Bonds) ETFs. You can find bond ETFs to accommodate Short-term, Intermediate and Long-terms as well as International government bond EFTs. You can trade Leveraged Bond ETFs, Mortgage-Backed Bond ETFs and Convertible Corporate Bond ETFs, even Junk Bond ETFs!

5. Can I hold Commodities and Precious Metals in ETFs?

Well, you can't hold the actual physical product but you can hold shares of ETFs that store gold bullion, or companies that mine/ produce and sell commodities, as well as ETFs that hold options and futures of precious metals and commodities.

CHAPTER 21

Reasons to Learn to Love ETFs

Are you still scratching your head while attempting to trade single stocks? Or are you paying massive fees for poor-performing mutual funds? Read on to see why ETFs are the answer to your prayers:

1. ETFs are diversified; one fund (with one transaction fee) holds dozens, even hundreds of stocks. You've got choices without being overwhelmed with the details of individual companies.

2. An index fund doesn't suit your needs? Find the right sector fund. Want more leverage? There's a fund for that. Instead of buying on margin (a "No No" in IRAs and many 401k's; you can buy a leveraged ETF (*caveat emptor;* these ETFs have risks you need to understand before you buy).

3. ETFs are transparent. It's quick and easy to find out exactly what's in an ETF. Go to the provider's page or to sites like Yahoo! Finance or Morningstar.

4. You can sell an ETF whenever you want (when the markets are open). Mutual funds are priced once a day at the end of the day, and some limit the number or frequency of your trades. ETFs are continually priced and you can trade them just like you would a stock.

5. ETFs go hand-in-hand with a trend following strategy. Mutual funds tend to have investment minimums and early redemption fees that can leave your portfolio hurting if you don't want to

buy and hold. ETFs have no such restrictions, making them an ideal companion for a simple strategy. Be careful, though, and watch those commissions.

6. ETFs are tax efficient. Because ETF shares are created differently and no cash changes hands in this process, ETFs are highly tax efficient and rarely shoot off capital gains.

7. ETFs are cheap. On average, ETFs cost less than most mutual funds. But beware: some mutual funds are cheaper than similar ETFs, so do your research to ensure you're getting the best deal.

8. You have choices galore. Commodities, currencies, emerging markets, exotic hedge fund strategies, active management, and more are available via ETFs. And that's on top of the wide array of sector ETFs available. Not long ago, only institutional investors had exposure to things like commodities and currencies; now you can have it, too.

9. ETFs give you power. You, the investor, have control when you're using ETFs. You can choose your level of exposure (broad or narrow), you can choose your sector, you can compare funds on key points and choose from several competitors. The growth of the ETF industry has really helped put the control back in the investors' hands.

10. ETFs have brains. The vast majority of ETFs passively track indexes, but we're now seeing more actively managed funds come to market. Actively managed ETFs give investors transparent access to an experienced manager, but at a lower cost than mutual funds.

The more you learn about ETFs the more you will love them as I do. If you want to know more about ETFs go register at www.howtotradebonus.com. One of many training videos you will find in your bonus sections is "Why ETFs".

CHAPTER 22

Lies and Myths About Markets and Trading

About the stock market

MYTH: Long-term Investing Is Buy and Hold

FACT: The market's meltdown in 2008 restarted the debate about the merits of buy-and-hold investing vs. timing the market. But, when using ETFs as part of your strategy, you have a third option.

The buy-and-hold (or BH&Pray as I call it) side continues to claim that no one can beat the market over an extended time, so a long-term plan, counting on the fundamentals of your chosen companies to increase the value of their shares and pay dividends, will lead to eventual rewards. They argue that predicting short market bursts is basically impossible, and they believe that long-term investing provides better numbers.

Even considering the recent market downturn, people who invested during the 1980s and 1990s are significantly up from when they first started investing, assuming they've been able to stomach holding and even buying during the major market downturns of this decade. That's a big if according to recent studies that find most buy-and-hold investors panic and sell at the bottom and jump back in near the top.

Even the world's most famous buy-and-hold investor, Warren Buffet, only buys when prices are a value, and he has been known to sell when he believes his stocks are over-valued. In addition, he is privy to information the average investor or even professional money managers will never have; CEOs take his calls. And, he buys enough stock to get a seat on the board and a say in how the company's run; often he buys the entire company.

The market-timing side points to the fact that many investors who've held on to their investments are now realizing they'll need to be part of the work force for quite a bit longer than they expected. This part may be true; many investors lost 40, 50 percent or even more during the 2008 crash and have yet to recover. That's because **to recover from a 40 percent drawdown takes a return of 67 percent, and to recover from a 50 percent loss you need a 100 percent gain**. Some of those investors have had to delay or call off retirement entirely and for the rest, making up that lost ground could take years.

MYTH: Invest Long Term in Good Companies for Above Average Returns

FACT: For much of the 20th century, it was prudent to invest your money in the stocks of a few good companies whose market value reflected the business's growth and who shared the profits as dividends with their shareholders. But today's market is a much more volatile environment for individual stocks; good companies can experience sudden, unforeseen problems that can tank their stock price by half or more in a just a few weeks. And, the definition of a good company changes over the economic cycle, as management comes and goes, and mergers and buyouts occur. And, as we've seen recently with the banking sector, dividends can be cut drastically or eliminated altogether at the discretion of management.

Institutional traders or people with large portfolios who hire professionals do better with stock market timing. They're in the markets daily, have insider knowledge, control significant market resources, and use advanced strategies created by specialists and executed by computerized trading. Market timing and buying-and-holding are two extremes. You do have a third option: trend following. With a relatively simple strategy that minimizes the chances that your emotions will enter into the trade decisions, and a good money management plan, trend trading offers the opportunity to reap significantly larger returns than buy-and-hold to those without the resources to buy a seat on the exchange.

MYTH: All Risk Is The Same

FACT: Most investors fail to distinguish between good risk and bad risk. Good risk is known as market risk, which is the risk that is inherent to investing. It's good because equity or asset investors receive higher returns than debt holders (usually); and investors are compensated appropriately for taking on market risk.

Bad risk is unnecessary; examples of this type of risk include sector risk and manager risk. Investors with portfolios concentrated in just a few stocks or market sectors take on sector risk. Those who invest in actively managed funds in which fund managers are employing subjective decision making take on manager risks and often pay a heavy price when their manager's style conflicts with market conditions.

MYTH: "This is a good time to invest in the stock market."

FACT: Really? Ask your broker when he warned clients that it was a bad time to invest. October 2007? February 2000? A broken watch tells the right time twice a day, but that's no reason to wear one. Or as someone once said, asking a broker if this is a good time to invest in the stock market is like asking a barber if you need a haircut. "Certainly, sir — step this way!"

MYTH: "Stocks on average make you about 10 percent a year."

FACT: This is based on some past history — stretching back to the 1800s — and it's full of holes. About three of those percentage points were from inflation. The other seven percent may not be reliable either. The data from the 19th century are suspect; the global picture from the 20th century is complex. Experts suggest five percent may be more typical. And stocks only produce average returns if you buy them at average valuations. If you buy them when they're expensive, you do a lot worse.

MYTH: "Our economists are forecasting..."

FACT: Ask your broker if the firm's economist predicted the most recent recession — and if so, when. The record for economic forecasts is not impressive. Even into 2008 many economists were still denying that a recession was on the way. The usual shtick is to predict a slowdown, but not a recession. That way they have an escape clause, no matter what happens. Warren Buffett once said that forecasters made fortune tellers look good.

MYTH: "Investing in the stock market lets you participate in the growth of the economy."

FACT: Tell that to the Japanese. Since 1989 their economy has grown by more than a quarter, but the stock market is down more than three quarters. Or tell that to anyone who invested in Wall Street a decade ago. And such instances aren't as rare as you've been told. In 1969, the U.S. gross domestic product was about $1 trillion, and the Dow Jones Industrial Average was at about 1,000. Thirteen years later, the U.S. economy had grown to $3.3 trillion. The Dow? Still about 1,000.

MYTH: "If you want to earn higher returns, you have to take more risk."

FACT: This must come as a surprise to Mr. Buffett, who prefers investing in boring companies and boring industries. Over the last quarter century, the FactSet Research Utilities Index has even outperformed the exciting, risky NASDAQ Composite Index. The only way to earn higher returns is to buy stocks cheap in relation to their future cash flows. As for risk, your broker probably thinks that's volatility, which typically just means price ups and downs. But risk is really the possibility of losing principal.

MYTH: "The market's really cheap right now. The P/E is only about 13."

FACT: The widely quoted price/earnings (PE) ratio, which compares share prices to annual after-tax earnings, can be misleading. That's because earnings are so volatile — they're elevated in a boom, and depressed in a bust.

Look at other valuation metrics, like the dividend yield, which looks at the dividends you get for each dollar of investment; or the cyclically adjusted PE ratio, which compares share prices to earnings over the past 10 years; or "Tobin's q," which compares share prices to the actual replacement cost of company assets. No metric is perfect, but these three have good track records. Right now all three say the stock markets pretty expensive, not cheap.

MYTH: "You can't time the market."

FACT: This old chestnut keeps the clients fully invested. Certainly it's a fool's errand to try to predict the market's twists and turns. But that doesn't mean you have to suspend judgment about overall valuations and give up any hope of profiting from market volatility.

Trend traders allow the market price, which reflects the risks and expected rewards of all the active participants and reflects all known information about a security, to dictate their entry and exit points. Instead of trying to beat the markets, they join and reap the profits without benefit of fortunetellers or luck.

MYTH: "We recommend a diversified portfolio of mutual funds."

FACT: If your broker means you should diversify across things like cash, bonds, stocks, real estate, commodities and precious metals, then that's good advice. Your total net worth should be composed of a variety of assets that are not closely correlated.

But too many brokers mean mutual funds with different names and styles like large-cap value, small-cap growth, midcap blend, international small-cap value, and so on. These are marketing gimmicks. There is, for example, no such thing as midcap blend. These funds are typically 100 percent invested all the time, and all in stocks. In this global economy, even international offers less diversification than it did, because everything's getting tied together (correlated).

MYTH: "This is a stock picker's market."

FACT: Every market seems to be defined as a "stock picker's market," yet for most people the lion's share of investment returns — for good or ill — has typically come from the asset classes they've chosen rather than the individual investments. And even if this does turn out to be a stock picker's market, what makes you think your broker is the stock picker in question?

I prefer to let the market pick for me, using ETFs, saving me the time and worry of picking individual stocks and being able to tell the future.

MYTH: "Stocks outperform over the long term."

FACT: Define the long term. If you can be down for 10 or more years, exactly how much help is that? As John Maynard Keynes, the economist once said: "In the long run we are all dead."

MYTH: Interest rates are the principal driver behind stock prices.

FACT: How many times have you heard that rising interest rates are bad for the stock market, and that declining rates are good for stocks?

Most stock brokers, and the majority of analysts and newsletter editors, espouse the same causal relationship between interest rates and stock prices. But the fact of the matter, the plain truth, is that there is no typical relationship between interest rates and stock prices.

Consider the last 10 years of stock market action. From March 2000 to October 2002, the Federal Funds rate declined from 5.85 percent to 1.75 percent, and the NASDAQ plunged 78 percent. Stocks and interest rates went down together.

From March 2003 to October 2007, the Federal Funds rate rose from 1.25 percent to 4.75 percent, and the Dow went from 7,992 to 13,930 — a 74.2 percent gain. Stocks and interest rates went higher together.

Contrary to popular belief, there is no standard relationship between interest rates and stock prices; we might even make the case that when interest rates rise so do stock prices (and vice-versa).

MYTH: Rising oil and energy prices are bearish for stocks. This is based on the assumption that the increasing cost of energy is a tax on consumers and reduces corporate profits as well. Therefore, rising energy prices are bearish for stocks.

FACT: There is no consistent relationship between energy prices and stock prices.

Sometimes energy prices are rising along with stock prices, and sometimes they decline together. The relationship between energy prices and stock prices, if related at all, historically tends to lean towards a positive correlation; like we've seen in the last year, for instance.

Since its low in March 2009 at 6,440, the Dow is up more than 65 percent. Simultaneously, the price of oil rose from a low in the mid-$40 range to $80 and above, an increase of over 75 percent.

MYTH: A widening trade deficit is bad for an economy, and conversely, a narrowing trade deficit is good and this is reflected in stocks prices.

FACT: The argument goes like this: A country is importing more than it's exporting, hence, it's shipping more capital offshore than it's bringing onshore. Therefore, domestic stock prices must go down.

But history proves that it is entirely wrong and nothing more than a myth. From 1976 to 1998 the U.S. trade deficit ballooned from $6.08 billion to $166.14 billion. And guess what? The Dow Jones Industrials went from 848.63 to 9,343.64.

In truth, the relationship between the trade deficit or surplus, and stock prices is exactly the opposite of what the pundits claim. A rising trade deficit is related to rising stock prices, and a narrowing trade deficit with recessions and falling stock prices.

MYTH: Corporate earnings drive stock prices. Another great, giant myth, perhaps even the biggest of them all: That if a company's earnings are rising, the company must be growing, therefore, its coffers must be filling up with cash to pay dividends, or acquire new products or other companies, and good times are here to stay. So the company's stock price must go up. Conversely, if earnings are falling, stock prices must go down.

FACT: Well, have you ever seen a company announce better-than-expected earnings, and its share price gets clobbered? I'm sure you have. Conversely, you've also seen plenty of companies announce lower-than-expected earnings, and their share prices move up. The same thing can happen to the broad markets, taken as a whole.

For example, 1973 to 1975: The combined earnings of the S&P 500 companies rose strongly for six consecutive quarters, yet the S&P 500 Index fell more than 24 percent.

And according to research conducted by analyst Paul Kedrosky, since 1960, the average annual return on the S&P 500 was greatest when earnings were falling at a clip of 10 percent or more. While the smallest returns on the S&P 500 occurred when earnings were growing at up to 10 percent per annum.

Rising corporate earnings do not guarantee rising stock prices, and falling corporate earnings do not guarantee falling stock prices. As a trend trader, I don't have to project and apply rules like this, I let the market price tell me when to enter and exit a particular stock or sector or market.

MYTH: An economy's GDP drives stock prices.

FACT: Most investors and most analysts agree, stock market prices as a whole, especially in terms of total market capitalization, should reflect a country's gross domestic product (GDP), the sum total of a country's overall economic output.

But consider the following: From the quarter ending June 30, 1976, to the quarter ending March 31, 1980, GDP rose in 15 of 16 quarters. Yet the Dow Industrials fell 22 percent. And from April 1, 1980 to September 30, 1980, quarterly GDP contracted, yet the Dow Industrials rose almost 19 percent.

About Investment Advice

MYTH: The Media is a Good Source of Investment Advice.

FACT: The media **does not** exist to provide you sound investment advice (nor is it obligated to). The media is in business to turn a profit, and that profit is made by drawing readers, viewers, or web visitors to their content and keeping them there as long as possible. This is only possible when the content is dramatic and emotional, and the principles of prudent investing are decidedly not dramatic. Wall Street is expert at feeding the media with the type of sensational content that hooks investors by appealing either to their fear or greed as dictated by the current market environment, thereby furthering its endless need to have individual investors in a constant state of buying and selling.

MYTH: Brokerage Firms Are Built On A Client Service Model

FACT: The big brokerage firms are built on a product-distribution model. The endless, massive fines those firms keep incurring for violating their investors' best interests testify to this fact. Brokers who are compensated by the products they sell cannot claim to be objective and do not meet a fiduciary standard of care for their clients.

MYTH: All Financial Advisors are the Same.

FACT: There's a tremendous range in quality based on education, certifications, experience, services, method of compensation, compliance records, conflicts of interest, and other important criteria. This substantial range in quality creates a major financial risk when you select an advisor.

MYTH: Advisors Must Disclose their Credentials and Business Practices.

FACT: There are no disclosure requirements. You have to know the right questions to ask to uncover the facts about your advisor. If you don't know the right questions, there is a high probability you selected your current advisor for the wrong reasons.

MYTH: Financial Advisors Must Meet Minimum Education Requirements Like Other Professionals

FACT: There are no industry requirements for education, not even a high school diploma. Other professionals who provide knowledge-based services, such as CPAs and attorneys, have substantial education requirements. Financial service professionals have none because they work in a sales industry and not a knowledge industry.

MYTH: Professionals Must have a Minimum Amount of Experience Before they can Provide Financial Advice.

FACT: There are no minimum experience requirements to be a financial advisor. Advisors can begin selling financial products the same day they receive their licenses. Another reality, the minimum age to be an advisor is 18.

MYTH: Only People with Clean Criminal Records are Licensed to Provide Financial Advice.

FACT: Individuals with criminal records can obtain securities licenses as long as their crimes weren't securities related. Although it may not be criminal, advisors with long histories of investor abuse are allowed to retain their securities licenses.

MYTH: Professionals Must have Appropriate Experience, Certifications, and Licenses to Call Themselves Financial Planners or Advisors.

FACT: There are no requirements to be a financial planner or advisor. Any professional can use these titles/roles whether they have the appropriate knowledge or not. Less scrupulous advisors use the titles to camouflage their real intent of selling financial products for substantial commissions.

MYTH: The Role of Planners and Advisors is to Help Investors Achieve their Financial Goals.

FACT: All advisors say that, but their principal motivation is earning good livings for themselves and their families. Then they have to produce enough revenue to keep their jobs and pay their business expenses. Only a small percentage of advisors are willing to put your interests first.

MYTH: Securities Licenses Mean an Advisor is a Competent Professional.

FACT: Advisors must pass a simple test to obtain a license. Special schools can help them pass the test after a few hours of study. **Licensing has nothing to do with competence**. It takes thousands of hours of education and experience to become a high quality financial expert.

MYTH: Professionals Who Work for Commissions Provide Free Services.

FACT: There are no free services. Commissions are paid by companies to compensate advisors for selling their investment (mutual funds) and insurance (annuities) products. This source of payment is a major conflict of interest. Plus, the real cost of the advisors' services is hidden because the product companies raise the fees they charge you to offset the commissions they paid your advisor.

MYTH: Nice, Friendly Professionals are Safe Choices.

FACT: The personalities of professionals have nothing to do with competency and integrity. In fact, advisors' personality traits can be a sales tactic, because they know you let your guard down when you like someone. Then it's easy to win your trust and assets.

MYTH: Older Advisors Have More Financial Experience than Younger Advisors.

FACT: Brokerage firms know you assume older advisors are more experienced. Consequently, they hire older advisors to create the illusion of experience. This is a deceptive sales practice. Do not equate age to experience.

MYTH: It's All About Past Performance.

FACT: It is one of the great ironies of investing that the more you make investment decisions based on performance, the more likely you are to experience poor performance. The reality is that the performance of stocks, funds and managers is usually attributable to what market sectors have recently been in favor. Since those sectors cycle in and out of favor quickly and unpredictably, investors who chase returns usually miss the run-up and arrive just in time for the downturn.

MYTH: Investors Do All Right for Themselves.

FACT: Do-it-yourself investors, without a strategic plan and process, are often plagued by cognitive dissonance – the brain's tendency to focus on the positive and block out the negative, which leads investors to bask in their successes and conveniently ignore their disasters. Investors also suffer from the modern malady that is the desire for instant gratification, churning their accounts in a fruitless quest for easy money. As a result, individual investor performance tends be much worse than what those investors realize, because investors don't adequately track the costs of trading and taxes. This lack of a true net performance number keeps them from having to face the consequences of their actions.

MYTH: An Investment Advisor's Job Is To Find You Opportunities

FACT: The most important role of an investment advisor is to bring discipline and resolve to the investment process and provide a barrier between your money and your emotions. Advisors who are constantly peppering you with the latest, greatest investment opportunity – be it fund, manager, stock , annuity, or whatever – are not advisors at all but merely product sellers in disguise.

About Trading

MYTH: Activity is Good.

FACT: Investors allow fear of the unknown to coerce them into making rash decisions with their investments. Those decisions are often encouraged by advisors (product-compensated sales people) who convince the investor that moving around to avoid/capitalize on current market conditions is wise. In reality, activity in a portfolio is usually detrimental and causes investors to miss out on the crucial few days of huge gains the market delivers, usually when we least expect it. This constant activity is the reason investor returns trail market returns by a wide margin.

MYTH: Making a Lot of Money in the Stock Market Requires Taking a Lot of Risk

FACT: While there are risks in all aspects of life, stock market investing actually offers the opportunity for long term, potential wealth for the average investor. Anyone who has the discipline and the time to learn the basics of stock investing may find that it is a lucrative way to amass wealth over time.

In many cases, stock investing may be less risky than certain real estate, commodity, or collectibles investing. Investing in your own business may be a greater risk than investing or trading in the financial markets.

MYTH: Only Brokers and the Wealthy Are Equipped to Succeed in the Markets

FACT: The Internet has made the financial markets accessible to anyone who has a computer. Background research, anecdotal data, and online trading are options for anyone with a computer and the desire to learn.

MYTH: Stocks that Are High Will Eventually Fall Again

FACT: Stocks that fall will not always rise again and vice-versa. Many factors determine whether the stock goes up or down in price. A stock's price is not just a reflection of how well the company is running its business but what the market believes about the company, the sector and the economic climate.

MYTH: The Best Time to Buy a Stock Is When Its Value Is Falling

FACT: If a stock's value is falling, it may or may not be a good time to buy. Generally, investors buy stocks with the assumption that the stock is going to increase in value. If the stock is falling, investor expectations are not being met. The best time to buy a stock may actually be when the stock is on the rise, because it is meeting investor expectations. Conversely, if you learn to short-sell you can profit whichever way the price moves. (**To learn more about how you can short-sell for profits go register for our free training videos at *www.howtotradebonus.com* You can also short sell using an IRA account by using basic options, we teach our members how.**)

MYTH: The Best Time to Sell a Stock Is when Its Value Is Rising

FACT: Again, a variety of factors need to be considered. If a stock's value is rising, investor expectations are being met. The stock may well continue to rise and trend traders use this opportunity to make money buying high and selling higher.

MYTH: Accurate Prediction Ability Is Crucial to Succeed in the Stock Market

FACT: Although it is easy to get caught up in the short term fluctuations of the market, few professionals are accurately able to predict market activity from day to day. Trend traders use the price as a guide instead of trying to forecast the future just observing the present.

MYTH: Young Investors Can Afford to Take More Risks than Older Investors

FACT: It is true that older investors (nearing retirement) should manage risk to preserve capital. But young investors, with time on their side, have large expenses looming such as buying a first home and financing their children's education. The Trend and Risk Control via Money Management is your edge to early retirement, no matter your age.

If early retirement is important to you learning to trend trade ETFs is the perfect low risk opportunity for you to do so. Once you put down this book before you get sidetracked go register for our free training videos and advanced money management software at *www.howtotradebonus.com*.

MYTH: A Little Knowledge Is Sufficient

FACT: In the realm of investing, a little knowledge may not be enough. If you want to manage your own investments, you should spend the time needed to learn to manage and trade your own accounts unless you choose to turn it over to a professional money manager (see Myths and Lies about Money Managers, above).

MYTH: Traders are Bred Not Made

FACT: Professional traders spend most of their time trading the markets, not marketing their services or teaching new traders. But it is possible to learn to trade the markets profitably by following the pros' example. In a famous example called Turtle Traders, a **group of inexperienced traders** were taught a system by a successful commodities trader, Richard Dennis, and during the next 4 years they made over $100 million in profits. Several of the trainees are now famous traders and trading teachers. This begs the question, ***"Why Not You?"***

First, at least 90 percent of professional traders manage other people's money. They do it because the fees they earn are substantially more than they can make just trading an individual account. Managing other people's money adds a lot of pressure and requires them to report their results which can help a trader maintain discipline.

The documented returns the pros make can be astounding. Years of 100 percent, even 150 percent returns are not unheard of. Years where they make 30, 40 and 50 percent are even more common. They also have losing years. The losses are called draw-downs. Every system has them; the trick is to manage the amount so when the winning periods come they more than make-up for the losses.

The draw-downs correlate with the returns. The higher the risks, the higher potential return and generally, the larger draw-downs. Banner years are often followed by draw-downs. You must have a system to control the losses in order to have an account to trade when the winning periods come around.

So can new traders, if they get a system that works, match or outperform a professional? NO, at least not initially. Learning to control your emotions, trust the signals, and place the trades takes time and experience. As you gain experience, if you're working a proven system, you'll begin to experience a professional level return. Most new traders only get there by working with a pro in a mentorship situation. A mentor helps the novice practice discipline and maintain confidence through those initial draw-downs and keeps his ego in-check during the big winning periods.

Want to know more about professional traders? I recommend these books for all new traders:

By Mark Douglas and by Jack Schwager:

They're entertaining, enlightening and a realistic look at professional traders.

You can also watch a video we put together showing the actual returns professional traders reported during the late 1990s into the 2000s at: *www.howtotradebonus.com* and click on "The most controversial trading video ever made'.

Few investors have the steely resolve necessary to stay the course, all the time, in every market environment. At some point in their investment lives, most individuals will allow their emotions to influence their investment decisions, a deviation that will result in lost future earnings for the investor.

The sensitivity of investors to bad news and fear of future events is exponentially greater today than it was in years past. Much of this is attributable to the endless, instantaneous transmission of news, which is distressing and overwhelming to the senses. The advent of electronic trading has enabled investors to trade on these fears and anxieties at a moment's notice. Your opinion about the state of the world, where we are headed and how fast we are headed there is a matter of personal perspective, but if you let negativity start influencing your investment decisions then you are guaranteeing a bleak future (at least financially) for yourself.

CHAPTER 23
You Need to Know: Trends and ETFs

Why trend trade ETFs

ETFs are the easiest and most profitable way to create a large portfolio and access various markets and sectors.

According to current data, about 68 percent of any particular stock's price movement is sector-related. When you start thinking in terms of trends and sectors, as opposed to individual stocks, you gain emotional control and mental clarity. No more feeling overwhelmed as you scan the thousands of publicly traded stocks and Mutual Funds. Instead, trend traders use ETFs to focus on and profitably trade the 46 sectors and a few indexes.

And, instead of spending hour upon hour trying to understand individual companies and what moves their stock prices, trading an ongoing trend will allow you to spend just a few minutes a day tending to your positions.

Fees will bankrupt your portfolio

Paying those "Professional Advisor" fees to an independent money manager or Mutual Fund manager, does not buy you better returns. You pay, regardless of whether their advice made you money or cost you. By some fairly conservative calculations, you'll pay 3.5 percent in various fees to a Mutual Fund manager each year. If your returns look anything like the S&P500's as of Dec. 31, 2008:

Timeframe	S&P 500	Minus 3.5 percent fees
1 year	(37.0 percent)	(40.5 percent)
3 years	(8.4 percent)	(11.9 percent)
5 years	(2.2 percent)	(5.7 percent)
10 years	(1.4 percent)	(4.9 percent)
15 years	6.5 percent	3.0 percent
Since inception	8.4 percent	4.9 percent

Paying 3.5 percent every year leaves you losing the battle to inflation and even suffering principle erosion. Not only that, you have to gain more than 68 percent to recover the 40.5 percent loss.

Fundamental analysis vs. the fortune tellers

I call it fuzzymentals. Academics use it to try to predict the future market price with what's happening to the company, the industry, the economic climate, government intervention, even the weather. I'm not saying that these don't factor into the market price, in fact I'm saying that all the variables have been accounted for and are reflected in the market price.

Almost all successful traders use technical analysis. The first problem with fundamental analysis is that it's difficult to obtain accurate fundamental data. While various governments and private companies publish information and a myriad of analysts are ready with their opinions, the numbers are gross estimates and the analysts are wrong more often than they're right. With the global marketplace, even if you could obtain accurate current information, it would still be impossible to predict supply and demand with enough accuracy to make trading decisions.

Using technical analysis, based solely on the market price, we can start to see the trends that repeat themselves over and over again and take advantage of them to make money for our portfolios. We don't really care what the reason (fundamental) for the price movement is; we only care about identifying it and profiting from it.

Technical analysts argue that since the most knowledgeable commercial participants are actively trading in the markets, the current price trend is the most accurate assessment of future supply and demand. If someone is correct saying that for fundamental reasons prices will likely move up strongly in the future, the market participants who have the greatest knowledge and influence are already moving the price up now. If price is moving down, a lot of very knowledgeable people, willing to invest their own capital, must think price in the future will be down.

For this reason, almost all successful traders learn to follow price action and not try to predict turning points in advance. They trade with the large participants who move the markets.

Let's say you don't believe me that you think we should gather all the data that may affect the value of the stocks in an ETF. Even if we know all the insider and external factors, we still have no idea how the market is going to react. We may think we know and even be right about the direction but the height or depth or length of the reaction is almost impossible to predict from the fundamentals.

In his classic book, Technical Analysis of the Futures Markets, John Murphy summarizes the rationale for technical analysis this way:

> *"The technician believes that anything that can possibly affect the market price of a commodity futures contract—fundamental, political, psychological or otherwise—is actually reflected in the price of that commodity. It follows, therefore, that a study of price action is all that is required. By studying price charts and supporting technical indicators, the technician lets the market tell him which way it is most likely to go. The*

chartist knows there are reasons why markets go up and down. He just doesn't believe that knowing what those reasons are is necessary."

Technical analysis isn't 100 percent right on every trade either. But it's right often enough that when combined with good risk management we can take three percent or more in profits each month without spending our lives studying stock markets and the companies that issue the stock.

The proof is in the numbers

How long has it been since you did a personal assessment of your portfolio? Do you know what your net worth is and how it's changed over the last year, the last decade?

If you're on track with your current strategy, then stick to what you've been doing; but if your results are flat or negative, perhaps you should try something new. After all, aren't we all doing this for one reason? We want to make enough money to enjoy a pleasant retirement and not work ourselves to death before we get there.

If you are completely satisfied with your current retirement strategy, if what you are now doing is working perfect for you and your family and you are completely satisfied with your current retirement strategy, then **DO NOT** go to *www.howtotradebonus.com* and register for our free training videos.

CHAPTER 24

Trade Your Way To Wealth Action Guide

Let's assume I've convinced you to take charge of your portfolio and your future. Where do you go from here?

The way I see it you have two choices (three if walking away and doing nothing is an option).

1. You can continue to gather information and get educated about the markets and trading. Knowing the history, the players and the options will help you understand the markets better, but it won't make you any money. To help you with this, we publish a free newsletter and make a lot of videos freely available to anyone who requests them.
2. You can take action. To make a real change in your portfolio and your future you've got to start putting the knowledge into practice. When you decide to take Action you have a couple of decisions to make.
    a. You can go it alone, figuring it out as you go along, basically attending the school of hard knocks. I'd like to think that you've got at least a head-start with the information in this book and that you will, over time, figure out how to profitably trade ETFs. To get started, you're going to need a brokerage account. I have a couple recommendations (I receive no compensation from any of my recommended firms).

Open an account at either **Trade Station of Think or Swim**, fund it with some trading money, and see how it goes. Please remember our money management rules and never risk more than 2 percent of your trading portfolio on any one trade.

b. Or you can let me help you some more. I do have a program with detailed instructions, daily trading reports and twice weekly interactive web based classes.

You will receive the DVDs and workbooks in the mail within a week and during that time you can open your brokerage account and download the free charting software I recommend. It's up to you of course, pay at the school of hard knocks or pay a small amount for our ongoing assistance.

The only option I discourage you from taking is the wait and see, gather more information (it's a bottomless pit in the trading world) choice #1 above or to give up thinking you'll never be able to take control of your finances and your future.

Whichever ACTION option suits you, I hope you'll keep in touch throughout and share the journey to the life and retirement of your dreams with me and my mentees. Please call or email with any questions or comments. I always enjoy hearing from my readers.

Helping you retire on time,

Anthony Lowell

P.S – If you want to join our mentorship program now, you might have to wait as we only accept new students a few times year. Register at the site below to see if we are open at this time.

All trading involves risk. Read our full risk disclosure on www.howtotradebonus.com